Critical Communications
AN OPERATIONS GUIDE FOR BUSINESS

Critical Communications
AN OPERATIONS GUIDE FOR BUSINESS

BY
SAM MULLEN

PennWell Books
PennWell Publishing
Tulsa, Oklahoma

Contents

Tables & Figures

Dedication

With I love and respect to

Samuel Mullen, Sr.
Virginia L. Mullen
Marie P. Mullen
Samuel Mullen, III
Eric R. Mullen
Sandra M. Mullen

Acknowledgments

The following people have inspired me to write and have helped to educate me on the fine art of communications:

Paul Biggers
Ed Boud
Ben Damsky
Bill Eitnier
Mabel Miller
Elizabeth Stanger

I would like to thank the fine people at PennWell Books for their assistance in editing and publishing *Critical Communications: An Operations Guide for Business.*

I would also like to thank and acknowledge the Literacy Volunteers of America for allowing me to be a volunteer literacy tutor for illiterate adults, and for their continued research and progress in fighting illiteracy in America.

Foreword

Critical Communications: An Operations Guide for Business was written for people with direct responsibility for the success or failure of core business and support operations in organizations. These core operations have one pivotal characteristic in common: precise communications (or *mission-critical communications*, as they are known to my clients) must take place. It means that the sender of any message must compose it with care and deliver it in a way that will produce a desired result, even if that result is to do nothing for the present time.

The practice of mission-critical communications (MCCs) does not lend itself to good intentions or chance. MCCs are part of the overall design of a mission-critical service or process. A doctor giving orders in an emergency room, a fighter pilot receiving orders to fire ordnance at a target, a power plant supervisor giving orders to scram a reactor, a power system dispatcher giving emergency instructions to a technician in a substation, and similar tasks that parallel these in importance are all examples of MCCs. The fact that peoples' lives may be at stake is a common characteristic of the kinds of tasks identified with MCCs. More often, however, the fate of millions of dollars in equipment and other resources, possible environmental damage, or, perhaps, the organization's survival may be at stake.

This text will introduce the reader to MCCs in a concise format that should make it an excellent resource as supplementary reading to a larger volume on contemporary communications or for group work in a seminar. Through practical examples, the reader will examine the forces at work in the MCCs environment, wherever it may be. Such issues as how management might introduce MCCs practices in the workplace and what mission-critical workers can do to maintain those practices will be addressed.

A model will be introduced for helping to explain the process of MCCs. There will also be a discussion on methods for training mission-critical communicators. Advances in communications technology can affect MCCs, so the book will touch on how users of that technology can avoid pitfalls that can lead to serious incidents.

Damaging events have become commonplace in today's technical society, and have stricken organizations and society the world over. As we seek to lessen the severity of these events, one point is clear: effective communications plays a pivotal role in operations in any environment.

The lack of effective communications exacerbated such events as the Bhopal chemical release, Valdez oil spill, space shuttle Challenger disaster, the Northeast Blackout, Three Mile Island and Chernobyl nuclear incidents, and recovery from the numerous natural disasters experienced in recent years. If scientists and engineers, for example, are not skilled communicators, they can expect to spend more time defending their actions during and after damaging events.

A number of books, papers, and magazine articles have been written on the new "information society" and the growth of the "knowledge worker." Companies are reorganizing and downsizing operations to meet the challenges of 21st century competition. There is no question that MCCs will play a vital role in both the transformation and survival of organizations. More so now than ever before, workers need to be able to communicate effectively in all forms, including verbal, written, and the various types of electronic communication used today. With fewer people doing a larger share of work in critical areas of company operation, even inexperienced workers will have to shoulder a higher level of responsibility, and they will have to explain their actions to others who are under the same pressures to perform.

Manufacturers engaged in developing electronic control and monitoring systems will have to implement a growing information base of design criteria into the new systems. The specification of each new system will carry with it the obligation to meet the user's specific and growing needs. In the future, there will be less time to debug new systems and no system will be of much practical use if the operator must go through a rigorous process to retrieve information.

A few years ago, hypertext and multimedia software tutorials and on-line help were options; today they are expected. In-depth paper reference manuals for new systems will be more readily available in electronic form on compact disc. Intuitive references are growing more graphical in design, employing clear diagrams and charts. They will be designed to get users up to speed on a problem or process in less time than through traditional means, such as reviewing a thick technical manual.

This book provides an insider's view of transactions that take place in industry, as they contribute to either functional or dysfunctional operation. It also provides methods that can be implemented immediately to enhance communications for organizations that wish to pursue them.

CHAPTER 1

Introduction

What are Mission-Critical Communications?

Mission-critical communications (MCCs) are communications that are essential to the operation of an organization or are conducted by multiple organizations engaged in a common mission. They are in step with the survival of the organization. The organizations include any that operate in business, industry, and government, in any location or in multiple locations, providing essential products or services.

This is a broad definition that merits further consideration. But first, what exactly is meant by the term *mission-critical*? It is those communications that deal directly with making processes, systems, and procedures work as they are intended to work, within their specifications, and the transmission of messages and data that support these intentions. Examples will be introduced later to make the concepts clearer.

Readers may have been exposed to the fundamentals of communication; however, a cursory review of some essentials of communications will be offered through examples taken from real-life scenarios.

Proposed Audience for This Text

This book was written for the manager and skilled professional as well as the student of communications theory. It will help the reader build on systems and practices that have been learned through experience or through formal study.

Objective

The main objective of this book is to offer effective methods and practices for communicating in a mission-critical environment. Concepts are introduced through the use of realistic examples, which help the reader understand how to implement MCCs. The hope is that readers will practice these methods, thereby reducing exposure to problems caused by ineffective communications in mission-critical situations.

For many people, the language of MCCs is terse. Some readers may believe that people must take on an nonhuman, machinelike persona in order to use it. In reality, your skill set will include new tools and a new way of thinking about communications. This may not win more friends, but it may someday save a life or avert the destruction of an expensive piece of equipment, which might have threatened the security of others.

If the book is used with these thoughts in mind, I anticipate the reader's success as a communicator and as an active player in the organization.

Enjoy it. Use it. Explore the possibilities.

Introduction and Key Points

- Mission-critical communications (MCCs) are any communications that are essential to the operation of an organization, or those conducted by multiple organizations engaged in a common mission.

- MCCs are critical to the success or failure of core business and support operations.

- MCCs are part of the overall design of a mission-critical service or process.

Chapter 1 Discussion Topics

1. Discuss the problems of communicating in today's environment. Think in terms of our global society, and how computers have changed the way in which we communicate.

2. What "systems" and tools are currently in place to help communicate vital procedures and rules to employees?

3. Discuss the problem of illiteracy and its affect on communications in mission-critical environments.

4. What are some of the ways that illiteracy problems can be detected in the workplace? Discuss how remedial work in communications and training programs can help organizations reduce risk associated with illiterate employees.

Never expect anyone to engage in a behavior that serves your values unless you give that person adequate reason to do so.

Charles E. Dwyer, Ph.D., President, The Swarthmore Group

Author's Note: Dr. Dwyer is also a faculty member at the University of Pennsylvania and its pioneering Dynamics of Organization program for graduate studies. Dr. Dwyer lectures on "Human Influence in Organizations."

CHAPTER 2

Mission-Critical Communications in Use

Who are the communicators and when and why do they communicate?

If you can identify the people who are involved in mission-critical communications in your organization, then you will be able to apply the information in this chapter to your work setting. As a quick exercise, it may be beneficial to write down the names of the people who are responsible for MCCs in your immediate work area, including a list of the groups or departments with which they work. On the same sheet of paper, list the circumstances for which they perform these communications. For instance, is it to perform a specific operation or process of some type? The point of this exercise is to get readers mentally involved with the communications that apply to them personally.

For example, if the reader were to work in a facility performing some type of emergency dispatching, he or she might write the following: "To dispatch emergency medical vehicles in the city of Milltown." Below this statement, the reader can be a little more precise and write something like the following: "To dispatch an Emergency Medical Technician crew in a fully equipped medical emergency van in the city of Milltown." It may also be beneficial to write down when these communications occur. Is it a 24-hour-a-day job, or do most of the transactions occur during specific time periods? Finally, the reader can list some of the conditions under which people must perform the work—Is it sometimes stormy? Is it late at night? Are shifts long with very few breaks? Think about several environmental and human factors that contribute to or tend to reduce the effectiveness of the communicator.

Purpose of this exercise

The purpose of this exercise is to encourage readers to think about who the players are, the reasons that they communicate, when they communicate, and what circumstances come into play as they communicate in the mission-critical environment.

Consider the factors that are involved every day. Perhaps the reader has heard coworkers complain about the conditions in which they are expected to do their jobs. Their concerns may be valid or they may be simply finding ways to let off some steam. Perhaps both scenarios are true.

Today's managers will probably do their best to ferret out the barriers to effective communications. But before they can analyze, they need to know more about the environment in which people communicate.

Where are MCCs likely to be used?

There is no simple rule for when or where MCCs are practiced, but there are places where they are practiced regularly. Some of those include:

- Power Plants
- Emergency Rooms
- Control Towers
- Control Centers
- Emergency Operating Centers
- Medical Laboratories
- Operating Rooms
- Chemical Facilities
- Dispatch Centers
- Scientific Research Centers
- Switching Stations
- Transportation Control Facilities
- Police and Fire Facilities
- Emergency Management Facilities
- Government Facilities

When readers study the possibilities, they often come to realize that more facilities practice MCCs than they first imagined, and that number is growing every day. Technology has brought with it certain dangers, which make it imperative that managers, operators, and technicians practice a specific set of transactions that foster safer operation.

The word *safer* is used because these transactions help to reduce the likelihood for error brought on by miscommunication. Applying the language of the job, or its *transaction set*, does not guarantee error free operation. Nonetheless many believe that it is safer than not applying it at all. The next section discusses the use of transaction sets, and how they can fit into the mission-critical organization.

Introduction to Transaction Sets

The term *transaction set* (T-Set) to describe the set of transactions that are accomplished through the application of specific language, and that are prescribed by management or some other governing body to meet the standards of the task or job. Those standards take into consideration such factors as: *safety, risk exposure, mandatory operation of a device or system*. The language works congruently with the job or task being performed in the environment. A Transaction Set Model is reviewed in detail in Chapter 3.

Does the transaction set ever change? It certainly does. Ideally, it is shaped with the application of new technology, new work procedures, and other factors. How do individuals keep in step with those changes? The fact is, they do not. This topic is discussed later in this chapter, but for now, readers will be acquainted with the concept using a case study.

Later in this text, several aspects of contingency planning and crisis communications are covered, which are communications that occur in the MCCs environment; however, they require the application of a different transaction set (in most cases) than is experienced on a routine basis. Priority codes may be a part of these transactions, which bear further consideration.

Whose responsibility is it to adhere to specific language?

Responsibility to apply a specific language (and transaction set) on the job is assumed by the people assigned to the MCCs environment. They are expected to apply the language without significant variation. Of course, this begs the question, Why are some people more likely to need specific transaction sets on the job while others do not? This issue is also explored later on in this chapter.

What are the problems that communicators encounter?

An example of a problem that is sometimes encountered in electric utilities is presented here. Electric utilities routinely perform switching at substations to de-energize power lines in order to perform maintenance on them, such as having a line crew change out strings of broken insulators. In electric systems, power lines are terminated at substations where they are connected to circuit breakers and disconnect switches. (Figure 2-1). The switches are opened in order to de-energize a "live" electric circuit (one that is carrying electric energy). In substations that are controlled by people who have been trained to perform switching (as opposed to being controlled by a remote computer), a switching person will take instructions over the phone or radio from a supervisor who is located at a dispatching center or control center, which is a facility used to direct operations. A sample dialogue is offered below:

> The supervisor is on the phone with the switching person[1], who is located in a substation. A phone rings in a control or dispatching center where a supervisor is on duty. His task in switching is to supervise the operation of any device within his purview on the electric system.

SWITCHING PERSON: Hello, Is this Phil? Sounds like you. This is Sam at Newport substation.

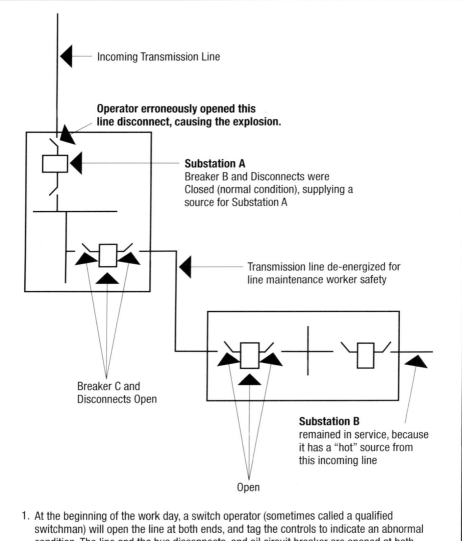

Incoming Transmission Line

Operator erroneously opened this line disconnect, causing the explosion.

Substation A
Breaker B and Disconnects were
Closed (normal condition), supplying a
source for Substation A

Transmission line de-energized for
line maintenance worker safety

Breaker C and
Disconnects Open

Substation B
remained in service, because
it has a "hot" source from
this incoming line

Open

1. At the beginning of the work day, a switch operator (sometimes called a qualified switchman) will open the line at both ends, and tag the controls to indicate an abnormal condition. The line and the bus disconnects, and oil circuit breaker are opened at both ends (terminals) of the line at Substations A and B, isolating the transmission line for the safety of the line crews. At the close of the work day, the line is restored to service by closing the switches.
2. With both sources open, after the operator opened the wrong switch, Substation A was put out of service. Customers fed out of Substation A were therefore interrupted.
3. Diagram simplified for case study.

Figure 2-1: The Switching Case Study (fictional)

SUPERVISOR: Yes, Sam, it's Phil. Did you check the substation when you arrived?

SWITCHING PERSON: Yes, I looked it over pretty well. Didn't see anything abnormal. You want to go ahead with this switching?

SUPERVISOR: As long as you looked everything over, I guess we can go ahead. Got your switching instructions handy? Start reading them off, Sam.

SWITCHING PERSON: Yes, Phil, got them right here. Let's see. On permit number 327 for Bill Roman; on the Clarkville 69 kV OCB C: You want me to remove red tags, close the bus and line disconnects, and then set to manual and close the 69 kV OCB C, and check it closed. Then I'll give you a call with the time. Okay?

SUPERVISOR: Okay, sounds good. Give me a call when you get through.

The switching person hangs up the phone and heads out into the switch yard to perform the switching assignment. The supervisor hangs up the phone and notes the time. He will now wait for a call back from the switching person, and will go over the switching he has performed.

The switching person, who had worked for the utility for 28 years, was very familiar with the job that he was about to do. He had been trained and he knew the substation very well. He had performed switching many times before at this location. The switching person was knowledgeable about the equipment that he was about to operate, which, in this case, was an oil circuit breaker (OCB) and a set of disconnect switches on a terminal point of a 69,000 volt transmission line. The line was dead (de-energized) because switches were open on both ends of the line. (Similar to turning off a light switch in your house. There is no other source for the electrical current to energize the light bulb, except through the switch.) His job was to close the switch at one end of the line, which would energize it from the "hot" (energized) substation source.

However something dangerous occurred in the next moment following their conversation.

After the switching person put down the phone and headed out into the switchyard to close the disconnects and then the circuit breaker, his mind drifted to his teenage son, with whom he had a terrible argument the night before. Following the argument, he had driven his truck down to Ed's Tavern and pounded down six glasses of beer. Feeling guilty and a little tipsy, he went home but he could not sleep. At 6:30 a.m. he had climbed into his truck and headed to work with no sleep. His son had packed his bag and left home.

As soon as those thoughts crept into his mind, they put him into a trance that made him forget what he was instructed to do at the substation. Instead of closing a circuit breaker, he opened a disconnect switch in a different part of the substation, where he had no business going. Because the switch he operated was not rated to interrupt the electrical current it was carrying, it blew up in a ball of fire, raining hot metal down on him, and causing an explosion that damaged more than one million dollars worth of equipment in the substation. The incident interrupted service to 5,000 homes for 12 hours. A piece of the molten metal came down and caught the switchman's shirt on fire. He received severe burns that nearly killed him.

The truth is, events similar to this happen around the world on a regular basis. They are part of the dark side of the complex world of interconnected systems that we build and operate. The devices and systems are built to be operated by trained individuals, using specific procedures, under specific conditions. There is no margin for the error brought on by a fleeting thought or a bad evening.

Charles Perrow probably said it best when he wrote his groundbreaking book *Normal Accidents*. Perrow explained that high-risk systems are "tightly coupled," which means that failed parts cannot be readily isolated from other parts in the system. Perrow described it as "...when an event occurs where recovery is not possible; it will spread quickly and irretrievably for at least some time. Indeed, operator action or the safety systems may make it worse, since for a time it is not known what the problem really is."[2]

An analysis of events, such as what occurred in the above switching example, often follows, in which data is collected and a case is written for review by those who may have some stake in the operation of power equipment. These lessons learned, however, may fail to hit their mark when translated into remedial measures. What follows may be overkill brought on by redundant procedures or, at best, a temporary fix.

Management's remedial action may by viewed by the people doing the switching as disciplinary in nature, instead of remedial. As a result, the new procedures may be resented by the switching personnel and, in fact, may be somewhat counterproductive. They may also be unsafe, because they may tend to make the switching person concentrate on the *reason* for the new procedures instead of the task at hand; of course, this is open to interpretation.

However, management is left in a difficult position as the result of such events, or so they believe, and something must be done above and beyond a discussion of switching safety with the people at fault. In the search for constancy in the fix, management often conjures up an entirely different or remedial set of procedures that may add steps to the process of switching in the hope that they will be interpreted as a message such as: "Slow down, follow procedures, and think about what you are doing."

Of course, the switching person and supervisor already know these cardinal rules and normally follow them. But, for a brief instant in time, something happened that they will never forget. When another switching incident occurs, it will remind them of their involvement with switching in years past it will surface in their minds again.

The supervisor will think about how he should have taken a few minutes prior to the switching to perhaps try to determine the state of mind of the switching person prior to asking him to do the switching. Perhaps if he had only asked the switching person a few questions, it would have given him an accurate idea of the switching person's state of mind. In turn, the switching person's answers might have led him to talk about his problem with his son, and the supervisor might have been able to help the switching person refocus his thoughts.

In addition, the supervisor might think to himself that he could have made the switching person recheck the substation and call him back prior to switching. By getting him to recheck the substation, the switching person would have familiarized himself with the setup of the substation, which might have reduced the probability that he would operate the wrong switch.

Then he might ask himself if he had communicated properly with the switching person. Were his communications on par with the transaction set that should take place on a switching assignment? Chances are, the supervisor will replay his conversation with the switching person on an audio tape recording, which is commonly used in MCCs environments. He will hear those dead spaces on the tape when something useful might have been said to possibly avert the incident. He will also hear the remarks that may have been outside of the scope of what was being done.

The transaction set for a switching task in an electric utility will include criteria to limit the use of language that is inappropriate for executing the switching task. Some of the objectives for completing each switching task are listed below.

- Dispatch of a qualified switch operator to the appropriate terminal on the power system. Order of switching sequence is important.

  Note: In the above case, we were talking about operating a circuit breaker in a specific substation on the power system. If the operator did not get accurate instructions on the location, for example, the switching transaction set would not have been compromised; however, the variables used in the transaction set would have been incorrect. This could have led to an incident, but it would have been averted most likely, because the operator would not have been able to locate a circuit breaker of the correct designation on the switching instructions. In order to set into motion an incorrect switching sequence, the operator would have had to: 1) arrive at the wrong substation, and 2) incorrectly identify and proceed to operate a breaker that was not on the written list of switching instructions—an unlikely event.

- Identification of abnormal conditions prior to performing a switch operation.

- A review of the instructions between the switch operator and the supervisor.

  Note: Depending on work rules, this could entail having the supervisor read the instructions to the operator over the phone, and having the operator repeat the instructions back to the supervisor prior to performing the switching. This double check is a common practice and has been effective in reducing potentially damaging incidents.

- Correct identification by the operator of the equipment to be operated.

- Checking off each step as the operator completes it.

- Upon completion, notification via phone by the operator to the supervisor that he has completed the switching, noting the time, and reading back the switching procedure as it was completed.

- Coordination of switching by the supervisor for restoring the opposite end of the line, where the same switching procedure will be followed.

When Communications Fail

When communications fail, that is, when people fail to communicate in a manner that fosters successful task completion, results can be far reaching. Sometimes communications fail as the result of assumptions made by the parties involved. Other times, the language itself is at fault, producing inaccurate pictures in the minds of the participants of what must be done.

When managers take remedial action following a switching incident, they are doing what they feel is best for everyone involved. Although, they may not be able to capture the real causes (events, feelings, thoughts, experience, conditions) for the incident, nonetheless they feel that some type of remedial action is in order. The action may not involve significantly more work, but the real issue is in whether management seeks input from the supervisor and switching person who have a stake in the work being performed. There have been cases in which the supervisor or switching person felt that because he or she was involved in the incident, management could not ask for suggestions on how to improve the process. In many cases, management simply asked what occurred and then wrote it down for the postmortem report.

Communicating and Thinking Visually

Another point worth mentioning with respect to communications that involve procedures is the concept of thinking visually. It has been said that we think visually, with pictures drawn in our mind's eye. When people are given a set of instructions, they may see themselves carrying out those instructions, stepping through each procedure to complete the task. They do not see the actual words themselves, but rather, the pictures that are conjured up by their interpretation of the words. It is therefore incumbent upon the sender to give the receiver the right words to help him/her draw those pictures accurately.

Successful task completion requires that we think rationally. In his book *Visual Thinking*, Rudolf Arnheim tells us that, "Thinking requires more than the formation and assignment of concepts. It calls for the unraveling of relations, for the disclosure of elusive structure. Image-making serves to make sense of the world."[3]

In no instance is this notion more evident than in emergency response, where words must be interpreted into accurate pictures for all responders so that further damage can be averted and lives can be saved. Planning and documentation consultants in industry are concerned with how words are used in the development of emergency plans, for example, and how they are visualized by plan users. They ask some of the following verification questions:

- How will this plan be interpreted by users?

- Have I clearly defined the scope?

- Is the plan organized to make it simple to locate information?

- Have I avoided unnecessary narrative?

- Are my terms clearly defined?

- Have I used diagrams effectively?

- Are there clear signs or criteria to trigger the user into action?

All of these questions help planners write the best plans for a client. The hope is that the client can then make the right visual images to carry out a successful recovery from an emergency.

The same can be said for almost any type of procedural manual, so we can consider asking similar questions during development. We must ask the users if specific wording conjures up the right interpretation of what they must do. Are they seeing themselves doing the procedure correctly? If not, the planner or writers must find the wording that helps the user of the document paint the appropriate images in his or her mind.

Successful Communicators at Work

Communicators who closely follow their transaction sets for given tasks tend to be more successful in their work. For example, when I was involved with the supervision of switching on the electric transmission system, I had the privilege of working with a number of outstanding people who performed switching at substations. In nearly every case, these individuals were excellent communicators on the job, at least when they were speaking to me.

Upon arrival at a substation, the switching people would call in and report any abnormal conditions. When asked to switch, they would jump into their roles as mission-critical communicators with ease. They spoke clearly, and with volume and tempo that made each word easy to hear and identify, even on those nights when the phones would crackle and hiss with interference. One such switching person was the best communicator of all the switching people with whom I spoke. He was calm and collected under the most extreme emergencies, and almost robotic in the way he approached every task on the telephone. He gave the impression that he was a strong individual emotionally and physically, and whenever a supervisor had him on duty, there was a greater sense of security.

Reviewing Job or Task Language and Associated Tools

Some key areas to review for job or task language criteria development for MCCs include the following:

- A review of policy and procedure manuals. Can existing language in the manuals lead to problems?

- A review of interpretation of the manuals. How are people using them? Are they using them? Why? Why Not?

- What are we teaching new employees about communications? Are we setting the right example? Are they conscious of their language on the job?

- Are our employees truly aware of the importance of following procedures and adhering to a concise, accurate transaction set?

- How can existing programs be improved as the result of this study?

- Are we in compliance with regulatory mandates?

- What are the key issues? (Prioritize them and set up action plans. Link them to organizational goals and benchmarking programs.)

Today's Environment: A Greater Need for Transaction Sets and Communications Training

As the result of the restructuring and reengineering going on in many organizations, many of the people who are excellent communicators are leaving. Where does this leave the organization in terms of mission-critical communications? Perhaps it leaves the organization very solidly in the remedial action and remedial training game. If people do not have viable transaction sets for critical tasks and the necessary training to implement them, industries are likely to have more errors and catastrophes that are solidly linked to poor communications practice.

One of the principal goals for writing this book is, therefore, to sell the reader on the concept of implementing a comprehensive approach to mission-critical communications.

Key Points

- The mission-critical communications environment can be found in many organizations. People in many parts of the organization may be regularly involved in MCCs.

- Technology has brought with it certain dangers, which make it imperative that people practice a specific set of transactions that foster safer operation.

- A *Transaction Set* (T-Set) is the set of transactions that is accomplished through the application of specific language. They are prescribed by management or another governing body to meet the standards of the task or job.

- Job standards, as they apply to T-Sets, take into consideration such factors as safety, risk exposure, and mandatory operation of a device or system.

- The T-Set for a job will change with the application of new technology, new work procedures, reengineering, and other factors. It can be revised at the same time a job is redesigned.

- Crisis communications require a modified transaction set that may include priority codes or other methods to differentiate them from routine T-Set language.

- Transaction sets should be maintained to help reduce risks associated with language used outside of the normal set.

- A switching incident case study was explored to emphasize the purpose and importance of maintaining transaction set language and adhering to procedures.

- When people fail to communicate in a manner that fosters successful task completion, the results can often be far-reaching and catastrophic.

- If we believe that people think visually, then we need to use the words that will help them draw the best pictures. People should be able to see themselves walking through a procedure, doing it without incident.

- Communicators who closely follow their transaction sets for given tasks tend to be more successful in their work, minimizing risk along the way for themselves and others.

Discussion Topics

Consider using the following topics to stimulate discussion in your organization:

1.   The role of transaction sets in the mission-critical environment.

2.   The need to enforce standard codes for the safety of employees.

3.   The use of transaction sets to minimize exposure to risk in specific areas of operation.

4.   Identify the people by profession who have the greatest need for using specific language on the job.

5.   What systems are currently in place for measuring the effectiveness of communications in the workplace?

6.   What training is currently being offered to enhance communications?

Each time you toss out a 'singing' greeting card, you are disposing of more computing power than existed in the entire world before 1950.

Futurist Paul Saffo, as quoted in the January/February 1995 issue of *I.D.* magazine.

CHAPTER 3

The Transaction Set Model

Model Defined

The *MCCs Hierarchical Transaction Set Model* (Figure 3-1) is offered as a model for introducing transaction set (T-Set) theory as we will explore it in this text. The bulleted text captioned above the model introduces some of the fundamentals of the model; more of them are discussed later in this chapter.

When a manager assigns a person a job, he makes some basic assumptions about the employee's ability to perform the job. It is a natural thing to do. Although some of the most gifted managers do it, they have gotten in trouble for making such assumptions.

This book takes the stand that mission-critical jobs and associated tasks require a more communications-focused approach that takes into account the following precept: In the mission-critical environment, job success (and hence organization success) is dependent upon transaction set design and implementation. It is therefore incumbent upon the job initiator or designer to ensure that appropriate and significant thought is given to transaction set design.

Most organizations do not have the luxury of assumption in mission-critical areas of operation. There is simply too much to lose. Subscription to this precept will mean that job design should include consideration of T-Set design, which will include specific performance criteria.

Performance Criteria

How will the T-Set designer develop performance criteria for the language that must be used in an employee's performance on the job?

The MCCs Transaction Set Hierarchy

- A mission-critical profession demands a specific *transaction set*, which is the set of all appropriate language and use of language, associated with the responsibilities demanded by that profession. It is shown in the model as *encompassing all job and task transaction sets*. As we show in the diagram, the job set does not include all of the language associated with a profession. For example, a nurse or an engineer can work in many different jobs, none of which would include all expected transactions associated with his or her professions.

- The *job transaction set* is the set that encompasses all *task transaction sets* that must be performed on the job. For example, we would expect a nurse who begins work at a medical facility to be able to take vital signs of a patient. The nurse may be asked by a doctor, "Take Mr. Johnson's vital signs," or "What are Mr. Johnson's vital signs?" The nurse then gives a response. These are acceptable transactions (using appropriate language) for the given task of taking a patient's vital signs while working as a nurse in a medical center. No matter where the nurse works, the set would likely be similar.

- As a result of a new practice associated with Task E, it now includes a sub-task (*labeled E' on the model*) that has made it necessary to include new language. This, for example, might be to write down an additional piece of information which will go in a log.

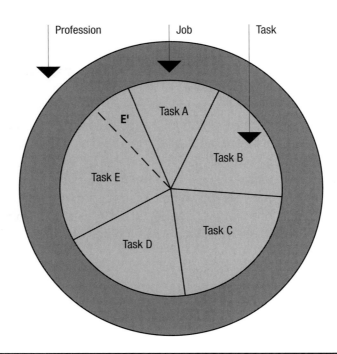

Figure 3-1: MCCs Hierarchical Transaction Set Model

Probably the most direct way is to look at task responsibilities and invite input on how these task will be completed. Obtaining input from people who are experienced in the tasks for jobs being developed is encouraged.

Let us look at an example of how this can be applied. If the switching example from Chapter 2 is used, we can examine a typical transaction for the switching person and write down a model transaction that could be used for switch operator training.

When operating a circuit breaker in a substation, the following could be an acceptable transaction set. (The transaction set does not include some tasks that are considered to be so fundamental that they are not included, such as, "Did you open the substation door?")

> The switching person or operator announces his location at the substation by calling the supervisor on the telephone.

SUPERVISOR: Did you check the substation? *(Connotation: Proceeding with switching at a substation that is set up in an abnormal condition could produce undesirable results, i.e., one could blackout or blow up the substation, or worse.)*

OPERATOR: Yes. *(Supervisor must get an affirmative response or operator cannot proceed with the switching).*

SUPERVISOR: Do you have written instructions for switching?

OPERATOR: Yes, I do.

SUPERVISOR: Please read the instructions.

> The operator will read the instructions, doing his best not to leave out any information. Pending an acceptable reading, and checking off each step as it is read by the operator, the supervisor will then allow the switching to proceed.

SUPERVISOR: You may proceed with the switching and call me back when you are finished.

OPERATOR: Okay, will do.

The operator then proceeds with the switching, checking off each step of the process on his form and writing in the time when the switching has been completed. He then returns to the phone to notify the supervisor that the switching was completed according to instructions.

The operator reads each step of the switching that was completed and reports the time of completion. The supervisor may then dispatch the switching person to the next assignment if appropriate.

The point of this example is to illustrate the disciplined approach required by T-Set design. Resolution of this process comes with the successful completion of the switching, which is more apt to be a reality if the T-Set language is consistently applied on the job.

Handling Distractions

The T-Set for switching keeps random conversation to a minimum so as not to produce distractions. Questions such as, How about those Celtics? may be great down at Dan's Grill, but they have no place in the MCCs environment. What to say is really a critical part of the T-Set model for switching on the power system. Distractions in any form can be instrumental in the failure of an individual to perform a critical task. This can be seen in assembly line work as well as work that may involve varied tasks. The reader has no doubt identified such noise and distractions in the workplace.

Critical Needs Introduced by the Model

The following needs are identified through the model:

- A profession that is applied in a mission-critical work environment is assigned a Job Transaction Set (JOB T-Set) which is a subset of a larger T-Set for the profession.

- The Job T-Set must be designed with as much care as is given the job design. Input in this process may come from experienced people who are familiar with the tasks for the job, including the communications that are appropriate in completing the tasks.

- As each task grows in complexity and familiarity, one can expect the employee to develop habits or tactics that will help him maintain the Job T-Set size. However, the employee may become overwhelmed as the T-Set grows beyond his expectations, perhaps due to increased regulation of an industry or other cause. This may cause as much frustration to the employee as the addition of the new tasks and responsibilities themselves. The employee may then find it difficult to execute the transaction that gets the job done.

- An employee faced with a radical T-Set expansion may seek more "releases" in the form of non-T-Set discussions on the job, which can lead to catastrophic errors.

Operating Within a Specific Job Transaction Set

Every mission-critical job in the organization, as determined by management, will have an associated design and job T-Set. T-Set design is covered in Chapter 4, but for now some of the basics of the model will be described.

As can be seen in Figure 3-2, a *job transaction set* is defined as the set of transactional language that produces success for the individual and the organization. If the job has its roots in customer service, then the customer must feel that the organization and the individual has met his or her critical needs. If the job is directly involved with technical work, including research, design, and operation, then the T-Set must meet the critical needs of the organization and its ability to produce. A scientist working in a pioneering research facility may, for example, work for

The Job Transaction Set Model

- The job is assigned to the individual who then assumes the *job transaction set*. This set becomes more familiar to the employee as he or she is trained, bu the employee must move along the learning curve of the job, including *learning the transaction set required to assume full responsibilities.*

- The transaction set for the job grows to encompass responsibilities outside of the set originally intended (as shown by the *dotted line* in the model). As some tasks grow in complexity, they force the growth of the transaction set for the job. This in turn forces the employee to learn (or keep up with) the terminology used in new transactions. The employee will only be effective at handling responsibilities if he or she can communicate with others. The new set must therefore be learned and practiced as soon as possible. The employee will likely be evaluated on the ability to master the new set.

- **Transaction set design** must be at least as well thought out as job design when new jobs are created or when existing jobs are being reassigned. If employees have a clearer picture of what the required job transaction set is when they assume their responsibilities,then they are more likely to be able to function effectively on the job.

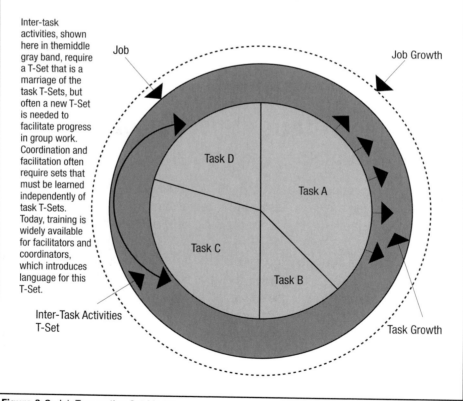

Inter-task activities, shown here in themiddle gray band, require a T-Set that is a marriage of the task T-Sets, but often a new T-Set is needed to facilitate progress in group work. Coordination and facilitation often require sets that must be learned independently of task T-Sets. Today, training is widely available for facilitators and coordinators, which introduces language for this T-Set.

Job

Job Growth

Task D

Task A

Task C

Task B

Inter-Task Activities T-Set

Task Growth

Figure 3-2: Job Transaction Set Model

weeks with a team of other scientists, using a relatively finite T-Set; however, when a discovery is made or when a new procedure has been developed, the T-Set may expand when a scientist coins a new term or a set of terms that will eventually be released to the scientific community. This occurs every day in the news and when a research paper is published. Scientists at work in other facilities performing similar work, will adopt this new terminology and it will become part of the job T-Set for scientists working in the field in a similar job. While other people will use the terms, they may not have direct responsibility for success or failure of an organization, and thus their use of the terms associated with the T-Set will be informative rather than operative.

The bulleted information above Figure 3-2 summarizes the major points of the model. When a task T-Set grows with added responsibilities for a task, there is an expansion of the T-Set associated with the job. Although it may be minute, we must realize that this can occur on a continual basis, expanding the requirements for a job T-Set by virtue of an expansion of task T-Sets.

Inter-Task Activities

The model in Figure 3-2 suggests that a common area exists in the T-Set, which is called the *Inter-Task Activities T-Set*. This T-Set is associated with group or department member interaction while engaged in group work. Without this area of consideration, employees would be less effective at handling group work that includes the completion of tasks with the overall goal of completing a project.

Examples of inter-task communications exist all around us. A number of successful training companies now offer an abundance of courses associated with coordination and facilitation of project work. Attendees are exposed to terms that are used in the facilitator's role in a group project. However, some groups may not have a dedicated facilitator on the team. That role may be left to a number of members who work to keep the project on course and on schedule. Those members will use language from task T-Sets as well as language that will meld tasks into successful project completion (which is a responsibility of the job). An example of this is given below in the hypothetical conversation among team members:

JOHN: I have completed the prototype of the user interface screen for the new plant emergency diagnostic program. I had to first get a feel for what the operator must monitor on a daily basis. Then I had to lay out the screen so the operators could get a good overview without leaving the first screen of the program. I had to deal with the user's needs and the fact that the monitor has only 17 inches of diagonal viewing area.

PAULA: As you know, I had to limit the size of the monitor to meet the physical constraints of an already tight control room and console area. It's the best we could do, John.

STEVE: I'm confident with your work so far, John and Paula, in each of your assignments. I believe we can move forward with the report generation phase next Tuesday. I'm looking forward to bringing in Dan Mitchell, who will give us more insight on report generation. It looks like both of you did a fine job at meeting the needs of the plant operators thus far. I'll have my update on the database work at Friday's meeting.

The above meeting scenario provided a practical example of the use of task-associated language and inter-task language among three individuals who are assigned to a system project. John was responsible for designing a user interface screen for a new piece of software used for diagnosing power plant emergencies. Paula, a hardware systems engineer, was responsible for specifying a monitor that would meet the tight physical constraints of the plant control room while providing enough viewing area for the user interface. Steve was responsible for database design work and acted as a facilitator and a champion of the project to keep it moving. The language he used let the other members know where the project was heading and that he appreciated their work on the project. Steve was using some of the language associated with inter-task activities, and hence, is part of the inter-task T-Set.

If Steve had used language that was clearly outside of the needs for the project at their meeting, a setback might have occurred, and Paula and John might have taken longer to resolve the hardware/inter-face issue. But Paula had done her best to specify the right hardware for the task and there was really nothing more that could be done. Steve was confident that Paula had researched all the needs and came up with the best recommendation for a monitor.

Steve, who was experienced in project work, knew that the group had reached a milestone in which another member of the task force could be called in for his expertise in report generation. He used language to enable the two other employees to look outside of their recent tasks and forward to a future milestone, which was to develop a report generator for the new system. John, Paula, and Steve were practicing appropriate task T-Set language.

In order to further illustrate the fundamental needs of T-Set design, Chapter 4 will provide cases in the mission-critical environment in which specific language is a requirement of the job.

Key Points

- The *MCCs Hierarchical Transaction Set Model* is offered as a model for understanding the relationships between job and task transaction sets.

- In the mission-critical environment, job success (and hence, organization success) is dependent upon transaction set design and implementation.

- Transaction set design can be developed with the assistance of organizational experts.

- Transaction set language requires self discipline. Familiarity with a task can lead to the use of language that is outside of the *task transaction set*, and hence, invites problems.

- The employee may fail to maintain a transaction set that addresses the growing needs of his or her job. For this reason, job design should take into account a growing job T-Set, which helps to assure that the employee will meet the growing needs of the job.

- The Job Transaction Set Model introduces the concept of job growth and the *Inter-Task Activities T-Set*.

- Inter-Task T-Set language can help critical projects to stay on schedule with minimal complications.

Discussion Topics

Consider using the following topics to stimulate discussion in your organization:

1. What are some of the methods that can be used to suppress the urge to distract others (and ourselves) with non-T-Set dialogue? How can this be presented in training other mission-critical communicators?

2. What are the likely events that may be experienced as continual expansion goes on at the task level for the jobholder as represented by the model shown in Figure 3-2.

3. What can a manager do to help alleviate the problems that workers might experience?

December 14, 1994, Washington DC–The federal government took the wraps off a new emergency alert system that will transmit information faster, emit a shorter warning, and require less intrusive routine tests over the airwaves. TV and radio broadcasters and cable systems will be required to install the new equipment...Eventually, TVs, car radios, compact disc players and other consumer products will be equipped to allow a signal to reach people even when they are not tuned in to these devices.

As quoted from a Reuters news article,
"New Emergency Warning System Developed,"
The Philadelphia Inquirer, 12/14/94.

CHAPTER 4

Job Transaction Set Design

Imagine the following conversation occurring during a meeting in progress at a crisis-conscious utility:

GEORGE: We need someone in the organization to handle our needs for emergency planning. And when a major storm threatens our service to the customer, I want that person to take control, to help us to get our emergency operating organization up to speed. What do you think about that idea, Janice?

JANICE: Yes, but we can't just put someone in the job and hope for the best. We need a pro who knows our operation. We need someone who can develop a plan and teach all of us what we need to do to be more prepared for emergencies. The applicant will have to be an excellent communicator.

BILL: We've been hit by enough storms and other emergencies in recent years to justify the position. More companies in our industry are being expected to have emergency plans and to practice them. I like this idea.

JANICE: Shouldn't we give that person enough authority to ask our managers to implement changes to get their departments prepared for emergencies? You know the drill, George, if the individual doesn't have the authority, people will keep doing what they want to do. No one knows how to prepare on their own. Many people wouldn't know where to start, and would keep putting it off.

GEORGE: You're saying that we need a full time planner/manager, and we need to give him or her enough authority to show the managers that we are serious about the notion of being prepared. Janice, you're in charge of the human resources area. Can your people work up a specification for such a position and have it available for us to review at our next meeting?

JANICE: We sure can, George. I've also been thinking a little bit ahead as we've been talking about this. If we give our new emergency program manager some training responsibility, he or she could teach our people how to speak with others and how to use telecommunications systems more effectively when emergencies occur.

BILL: This will help eliminate some of the problems we've had in the past with misappropriated resources and misuse of our systems. It's not enough to simply know how our systems operate. Our people need to be better communicators. We've been considering the application of transaction set design in our key operating positions. We can include language that will help people communicate during emergencies as part of their job transaction sets. Our new emergency program manager can help us with this.

GEORGE: Agreed. Let's move forward with this idea.

Developing Job Transaction Sets in the Organization

Job T-Sets are appropriate for positions in which people are expected to follow specific and direct communications paths in order to accomplish tasks that are critical to the mission of the organization. They represent clear thinking and effective action. Properly implemented, job T-sets can help reduce crises in the organization.

Table 4-1 introduces transaction set language that is consistent with the needs for a switching task on a power system, which was used as an example in Chapter 2. The transactions generally occur between a supervisor and the switchman or switch operator. The table offers simple examples of how language is used outside of the transaction set can be a source of problems.

Table 4-1: Sample Power System Operator Switching Task Transaction Set

Problematic Language	Problem Description	Transaction Set Language
1. "You checked the status first, didn't you?"	• Suggestive • Presumptive • Unclear needs • Device unspecific	• "Did you check the B switch controls status?" • "In which position are the 'B' switch controls?"
2. "Well, you checked the gauge before switching, didn't you?"	• Same as above	• "Give me the MVA reading that you recorded on Number One Transformer prior to switching. "
3. "This is Steve at the control center. I need switching completed on the 69 kV line we have out for maintenance."	• Same as above • Location unspecific	• "Please report to Smithfield substation and call me for switching." • "We will discuss the switching after you arrive."
4. "I'm here at Smithfield substation. The substation looks okay. Do you need switching on this breaker that's open?"	• Existing status of substation is unclear • Suggestive • Presumptive	• "Who is this, please?" • "What do you mean by 'The substation looks okay?'" • "Let's start over, John. Please take your time and give the substation a complete and thorough check. Then call me." • "I'll tell you what we need when you call me back."
5. "Are you folks keeping cool in the operations building? It sure is hot out here."	• Distractive remarks that lead to a non-task-specific response • Thoughts misdirected; not focused on work	• "Bob, I know it's warm out there, so I'd like to get right to the work we need to perform." • "Are you prepared to perform switching at Crestview substation?"

Language that is problematic can be identified by the trained ear. It is often suggestive, presumptive, and unspecific in content, and can lead to dangerous or catastrophic results. A few examples of problematic language are gven in Table 4-1.

The first example, "You checked the status first, didn't you?" is, of course, suggestive and presumptive in content. The supervisor may have made this remark to a switchman at a substation. Prior to switching, the supervisor would want the switchman to make sure that the substation status is normal; however, by presuming that the switchman had already checked the substation, he has asked the question expecting an affirmative answer. In a rush to get the work done, the switchman may simply say yes while he is looking around for abnormal conditions. This may or may not be the case, but the supervisor may never find out for sure, because he has, in effect, put words into the switchman's mouth. Also, the switchman may interpret the language as being demeaning, as if to say, "Did you do what you were supposed to do prior to calling me, or did you forget?"

The supervisor has not made himself clear in any case, because he simply said, "You checked the status first, didn't you?" The status of what? The status of the substation? A circuit breaker? A panel meter? The roof on the substation control building? Again, we'll never know until he makes his intentions clear. In our transaction set language, we do make it clear. We are specifically concerned with switch B, and more specifically, its position.

In Example 2, we discover some of the same language, which is presumptive and unspecific. In the transaction set, we were much more specific. We asked for a quantity in Million Volt Amperes (MVA) on a specific device—Number One Transformer.[1]

In the third example, the supervisor initiated a request to dispatch a switchman to a substation to begin restoration on a high-voltage transmission line that was taken out of service for maintenance. However, Steve assumed the person who answered the phone would know who he is (no last name given), and that the recipient of his message will know which line was taken out of service earlier in the day. These are dysfunctional assumptions for mission-critical communicators. The real source of concern is that language like this is practiced every day, in many types of high-tech industries.

In Example 4, the switchman told the supervisor where he was, but he assumed that the supervisor knew who he was since he did not give his name. The language that the switchman used would lead a seasoned supervisor to question whether the switchman had indeed checked the substation upon arrival. The statement, "The substation looks okay" is not a very reassuring way to tell anyone that a thorough check had been made.

Also in Example 4, the switchman appears to have assumed that he was summoned to do switching, because he asked, "Do you need switching on this breaker that's open?" The supervisor may have wanted the switchman to do something entirely different, such as provide a reading on a panel meter or check for an alarm condition in the substation. By making this assumption, the switchman not only envisioned himself performing switching, but also, that the switching involved a circuit breaker that may have been operated earlier.

The transaction set language for Example 4, shows that the supervisor assumed control of the dialogue and was able to bring into play the appropriate dialogue for the task. He refocused the switchman's attention on the language of the task, which is: "Who am I speaking with?" "Where is he located?" "What is he doing at the substation?" "If he's at a substation, we can't do anything until he has checked the status of the station." "Is anything abnormal?" "Ask him to perform a thorough check before anything else is done."

In Example 5, the problem of small talk enters the picture when important work must be done. In most cases, the remedy is a straight forward, back-to-basics approach—refocus the dialogue on the task at hand. Everything else is secondary. Look at the sample transaction set language recommended in column three.

Transaction set specifications can be drawn up in any organization and in any industry that is interested in improving its communications among employees engaged in internal and external projects. The design of job T-Sets is a straightforward process. Figure 4-1 may make this process clearer.

In Figure 4-1, one can see the (1.) criteria drawn up for the job Engineer II; and (2.) task and inter-task transaction sets, which will take into account the bulleted items listed in (1.) which are concerns for the position Engineer II. From the criteria, one can then look at the tasks (2.)

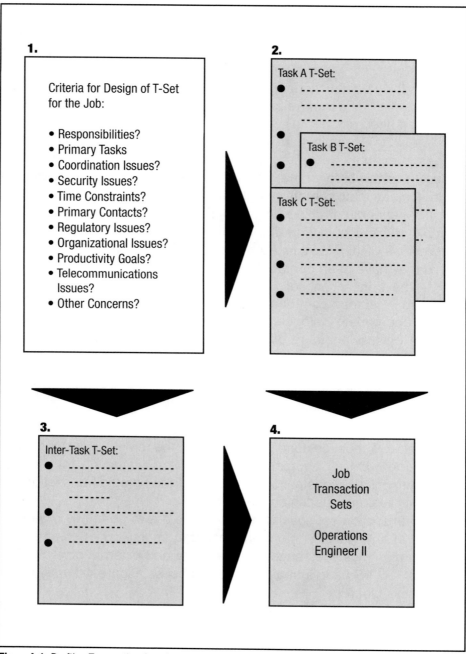

Figure4-1: Drafting Transaction Sets for a Job

that must be handled by the Engineer II, and at the language which should be used in the completion of the tasks. Of course, these are the primary tasks for the job, the ones in which we are most interested.

Experts from the engineering staff can then be called to assist in developing the sets for each task, or they can be sent a form to use in this process. Once completed, the form can then be mailed to human resources or another department charged with developing the job T-Set guide for the position.

With tasks mapped out, one can look at (3.) inter-task language, which can come into play in the execution of project work. If nothing can be put down for inter-task language, it can be saved for later evaluation.

Once the task T-Sets are in final form, they can be compiled in a useful guide or notebook (4.), which can be handed to employees as they assume the responsibilities for the position, much like they may receive an employee guidebook. For existing positions, T-Set guides can be developed with the assistance of the department manager(s) and experts for the tasks being considered. The employee can also be asked to assist with the development of the book, which may help generate the interest that is needed for full compliance.

The implementation of Job T-Sets is a sign that the positions being considered deserve special attention, and are clearly among the mission-critical processes of the organization.

Transaction Sets and Job Design

For each mission-critical job, a job design has been (or will be) developed. "Job design is the systematic process through which the work content, the rewards, and the qualifications needed is determined for the job."[2] If the responsibility for setting up, at a minimum, a preliminary transaction set for a job is added to the design, strides will have been made in helping to ensure effective communications practice for the new or transferred employee. Management will also have sent the message that they are concerned with the ability of the individual to communicate effectively on the job. The job T-set design can also be used as a part of the position description.

If, for example, during orientation to a job, the employee was provided with a notebook that outlines some preferred methods for handling specific tasks on the job, he or she could look forward to learning the job considerably faster. Granted, employees may be a little curious or even a little put off by the fact that people are telling them how to become more effective communicators, but if they look at it productively, they will benefit.

If a series of tables were placed in the notebook that outlined some of the appropriate language to be used for critical tasks, such as what was done with Table 4-1(2.) organizations could also look forward to a higher level of employee communications proficiency.

Some other important benefits that are likely to emerge from the use of an employee notebook are:

- It will help reduce the risk of a catastrophic event.

- It will contribute toward lowering the organization's exposure to risks associated with the work that is performed.

- Employees can help prevent others from contributing to a damaging event.

- Transactions will be easier to log, and information that is processed will be more complete for use in reports and postevent review.

- Employees will be more conscious of instructions to others, helping them to be more productive.

- Managers will have built-in criteria for evaluating employees' performance as communicators.

- Benefits will include clearer thinking, higher productivity, and more efficient use of telecommunications resources.

Job T-Sets: Maintaining Task-Oriented Dialogue

What has been offered here is task-oriented dialogues which can be thought of in terms of higher productivity and lower exposure to risk. It is driven, in part, by the constraints of the systems that are used on a day-to-day basis, coupled with the desire to use them in the most productive way.

In the examples, the language that was used is closely associated with system switching operations, and specifically, with the related mission-critical tasks that occur. Task-oriented dialogue can be "molded" to the systems in use in any environment by the mission-critical communicator. The power system example was used to stimulate thinking, and to make the reader aware that mission-critical communications are common to all of us, since all of us use electricity.

Making employees aware of their daily transactions can also help make them more conscious of the significance of communications in tasks and projects. If the job T-Set is extended to include language for response to emergencies, then the organization will also make employees more valuable as responders when it needs qualified people to solve potentially damaging and costly problems.

What to Remember in the Examples

The following activities, as presented in the models and examples, can be interpreted, transferred, and implemented in organizations to enhance communications in the mission-critical environment:

- Transaction set language that is appropriate for mission-critical jobs in the organization

- Peer group development of transaction set language that can may be incorporated into job design criteria for a given position

- Programs to monitor the performance of individuals who operate in the mission-critical work environment

- Global involvement in communications enhancement in specific areas of the organization

- Risk assessment reviews that incorporate communications issues

Key Points

- Job T-Sets are appropriate for positions in which people are expected to follow specific and direct communications paths in order to accomplish tasks critical to the mission of the organization.

- Properly implemented, job T-Sets can help reduce crises in the organization.

- A table describing problematic language (Table 4-1) was used to show how it can lead to incidents on the job.

- Control of the language can often be regained by refocusing thoughts on the work at hand.

- A diagram was introduced (Figure 4–1) to show how job T-Sets can be developed for various positions in the organization.

- *T-Set Guides* can be developed with the assistance of department managers and experts on the tasks being considered.

- Implementation of job T-Sets is a sign that the positions being considered deserve special attention, and are clearly among the mission-critical processes being carried out in the organization.

- When job T-Sets are developed, the message is sent to employees that the organization is concerned with the performance of the individual in communicating effectively on the job.

- Job T-Sets can be included with the specifics and standards expected on the job. Examples of task T-Set dialogue can be included in a notebook for the new or transferred employee.

- Practicing T-Set language on the job can help make the employee a valuable responder during emergencies.

Discussion Topics

Consider using the following topics to stimulate discussion in your group or organization:

1. Discuss the T-Set language that would be appropriate for one or more jobs in the organization, either your own or one with which you are familiar. To make the discussion more focused, pick a specific task that is performed by someone in that position. It may be beneficial to create an outline.

2. Refer to Table 4-1 and come up with a table that represents some of the language you have heard on the job that could lead to problems. List the problematic language in one column and the T-Set language that would help to derail a potential problem.

3. The diagram in Figure 4-1 illustrates the process of developing a useful, recommended T-Set for an Engineer II position in a company, but it could apply to any position for which a T-Set might be required. Discuss the people who might be involved in this process in the organization. How would they get the process started? What might the final product look like?

4. How might you investigate a serious incident that may have been attributed to dysfunctional communications? If you were a manager, how would you keep the incident from recurring? Choose an industry and a process, and describe how the process might be vulnerable to a serious incident. An example is an air traffic controller in a busy airport, but see if you can come up with one or more examples with which you are familiar.

It is becoming clear that crises are caused by overly simplified conceptions and fragmented perspectives in complex systems. As virtually all large-scale disasters remind us, broadening both our thinking and our feeling is no longer a luxury but a necessity.

Pauchant, T., and Mitroff I., (1992).*Transforming the Crisis-Prone Organization* San Francisco: Jossey-Bass Inc., p.47.

CHAPTER 5

The Communications Environment

Where We Work

Researchers have traced a number of environmental and human factors as contributors to some of the worst disasters in history. Therefore, in addition to being concerned with the quality of communications, which were explored in the first few chapters, this chapter will look at some issues that can affect communications in concert with transactional form. Some of the factors that can produce stress for the mission-critical communicator will also be explored.

Many people would use the general term *environment* to describe the conditions in which we communicate, including the location, and the features of the facility, such as lighting, sound, electronic devices, and hours of operation. In reality, the employee may be largely indifferent toward many of these factors, because they may have little to do with much of the work being done. More precisely, the employee may have little to do with specification, function, or design. But, of course, some factors have a lot to do with the quality of the work environment, and the security and well-being of the employee. Environmental factors play a major part in fostering a productive work environment, and also in contributing to conditions that foster catastrophic events.

A recent survey conducted in Germany by IG Metall, one of Germany's top 500 companies, revealed that 59% of the work force felt that the workplace had "deteriorated dramatically," and that between 30 and 50% of employees complained that supervisors did not take enough time to devote to their subordinates' personal concerns and, subsequently, to take appropriate action. It turns out that in seminars for the managers, the comment often was made that interpersonal relationships were not their concern; that it was not for their role to be "nursemaids."[1] These statistics are echoed throughout today's organizations. Denying that they exist simply prolongs their existence and makes managers less adept at resolving them.

Factors Over Which We Have Some Control

When employees do not feel secure in their workplace, the mission of the workplace may well be in jeopardy. The term secure in this study refers to a set of factors that make a worker feel as if he or she is on firm ground without the continual fear of management taking away his or her job without exercising fair treatment.

Many people have experienced a reorganization or reengineering in their company in which their position was eliminated, and can attest to the resulting increase in the level of frustration. While some employees are offered jobs elsewhere in the same company, this may not be a remedy. A feeling of mistrust clouds the office environment, and as much as management tries to get on with the work at hand, the employees often plan part of their workday around a job search, which may be conducted in subterfuge.

Many people have witnessed coworkers weeping, physically exhausted from the stress of replaying in their minds the scenario of being unemployed. They walked through the company buildings in trancelike states hoping to find a solution before next week or, perhaps, by the end of the day. Project task forces that would normally plow through work on projects often become stalled, with members worrying about what will happen if they say the wrong thing in a meeting where a superior is present.

Frequently one can see managers and upper-level management who know thay are about to receive their walking papers, and who are going through the same types of stress. Perhaps some of them are shell shocked, having laid off several people on their staff only days before. They must then deal with the remainder of their staff, who look at them with mistrust in their eyes instead of enthusiasm for the next project.

Although these are not the classic examples of interference to communications, they are nonetheless real and are common.

The effects of these issues hinder communications between employees who are normally very productive. As the conditions grow more common throughout the organization, the chance of a serious incident occurring also grows. The solutions are not always forthcoming. However, there are some steps that can be taken to mitigate the effects of some issues that involve communications, and are presented in the next section.

Speaking of Solutions

Words mean a lot. People react more favorably to less provocative statements from managers. For example, instead of asking a worker if she has completed a project, a manager might ask her for a status report. In this way the manager is giving her more control over the answer, which tends to put her more at ease. When managers ask employees to do something in the wrong tone of voice, or using the wrong words, some people react by going into a lower-productivity tailspin that can last for weeks or months.

An employee will continue on a less than productive course unless the manager is perceptive enough to pick up some of the subtle signs and attempt to remedy the employee's condition or attitude. However, readers may have witnessed precisely the opposite situation occur. Perhaps they have seen people at manager and top- management hold their heads down, eyes on the floor, as they walk down the hall of their office building. Employees can perceive this as avoidance, and not as a situation in which managers are in deep thought as they walk about. This kind of behavior contributes to poor communications practice. Employees want to say hello, ask a question, offer a suggestion, or they may simply want to bounce an idea off of someone who may care enough to listen.

What is often called "negative thinking" brought on by reorganization and layoffs does not have to prevail in organizations that are going through change. Managers have to admit, though, that they need better information before making a radical change, if that is the case. Calling in consultants may not be the answer either. Employees inherently mistrust consultants who appear to be out for the quick solution, especially when it involves layoffs. When organizations hire consultants, they should be prepared to explain the reason that the consultants have been brought on board, and do it in a way that employees understand.

In an interview for *Network World* magazine, Harold Nelson, director of the Institute for Whole Systems Design at Antioch University in Seattle, brings into play thinking that practically guarantees a more successful approach in troubled organizations. Nelson advocates the following approach:

> ...rather than try to escape a problem or get away from something that is broken, you begin to work toward something. Those two strategies are very different...if you are getting away from something, the only thing you're assured of is that you are moving away from it. You're not assured of getting where you want to be...if you work toward something and you have an idea about what you want, then you are guaranteed of getting away from what you don't want, and you're also guaranteed of getting where you want to be...turn your face where you want to go.[2]

Opening up communications in an organization involves mutual trust between employer and employee. The foundation for this trust must be sound and meaningful. It begins with communicating with employees before any radical change is made, and continuing with communications throughout the process. Management must ask the right questions, including the following: What other ways can we do this? Who needs to be involved? How can we help protect peoples' interests? Should change come as rapidly as some people perceive that it should or do we have more time? Will we be able to look our employees in the eye after this change has taken place? How can we ensure that the channels of communication remain open? People should not forget that when everything has been considered, communication may be the only thing that averts disaster.

Of course, none of these answers is easy to deal with when the climate for business has rapidly changed, but they are necessary questions for the crisis-prepared organization. Although the global view is not always the view of the president, someone must take it.

If the reader is a manager in an industry that handles a potentially damaging substance or product, seeing a reduced level of interaction among employees brought on by what many feel is a hostile work environment, is an indication to act. *The time to act is now.* The perceptions of people who must communicate in order to help avert disaster are critical. This is not something to debate with colleagues over coffee. It is real, it is global, and it is societal, and it requires the collective attention of management.

Researchers believe that fewer disasters would likely result, if organizations would take this approach. Instead of saying, 'It's a problem in our operations area' or, 'It's a problem in our fuel handling area' they need to say, 'It's a company problem, and we need to deal with it on a company level now before it gets any worse.'

What are employees saying these days? Are mission-critical communications working, or are people getting caught more frequently transacting critical operations outside of their job transaction sets?

Is management assuming that all is well with communications at the management level, or are they looking at communications objectively at all levels, recognizing successes as well as breakdowns? When managers find a breakdown, do they know how to handle it? These are critical questions for managers in industries today.

This section has looked at some of the emotional issues that can affect communications, other issues are addressed in the next section.

Fatigue in the MCCs Environment

Can a price be placed on the problems caused by lack of sleep in the MCCs environment? No, no more than a price can be placed on the loss of human life, which is the price of fatigue. But the real question is, Is the price high enough to get the attention it deserves? The answer is probably no.

Scientific data supports the fact that fatigue has been connected with a number of high-profile disasters in recent years.

It's a common but unrecognized thread that links the Exxon Valdez oil spill, the Challenger explosion, the Three Mile Island nuclear accident, the mistaken shooting down of an Iranian airliner by US Navy officers – and countless lesser tragedies on our highways and in hospitals, factories and businesses...the key people involved in these disasters were too tired and overwhelmed with data to make proper decisions, see trouble coming, react swiftly.[3]

The toll that sleep deprivation takes on people is devastating. Forty-million Americans suffer from chronic sleep disorders. Twenty to thirty million Americans have occasional sleep-related problems caused by rotating shift work, late preparations for business meetings and exams, or life stresses such as a death in the family.[4] Our 24-hour society is becoming more like a 36-hour society working in a 24-hour time frame, when it comes to the demands placed on many people.

These numbers hit home for the people who make their living on shift work. For a number of years, I worked shift work in a system control center at an electric utility. My responsibility was to monitor and control the high-voltage electric system, which affected the lives of about one million people. During the night shift, I worked with one other person. I can remember that at about 3:00 a.m.,on the seventh straight day of night shift, I hoped that nothing serious would happen, but often it did. A capacitor bank in a substation blew up at about 3:30 a.m. one morning, bringing the system voltage down so low that the alarm page on my computer was swimming with red (high-priority) alarms.

I jumped from my chair, bleary eyed, heart pounding, and brain foggy with lack of a restful night's sleep. I scanned the alarm pages of my computer, looking for equipment operations that would give me a clue as to what happened. With many high-priority alarms coming in, the sea of red alarms on my screen made it difficult to pick out the lines of code that would help me make sense out of the problem. At that point, I realized that it would take a long time before alarm systems would be user friendly for the night shift worker.

As a mission-critical communicator, my job was to make sense out of the computer data that was coming in and dispatch a technician to affected substations, where we would further investigate a problem. At the same time, I had to look at my load on the system, spotting any variation that would indicate a blackout condition.

Thinking to myself, I began to analyze the data.

Let's see, what's my system? What's my frequency? Any generators tripped off line? What does my interchange look like at my tie stations? (Most utilities are interconnected with other utilities to prevent a blackout for the loss of a generator or major transmission line.)

Any other circuit breakers open that shouldn't be? Okay, I'm starting to get a handle on this problem. It looks like a capacitor fault at a nearby substation, nothing more. I'll get a troubleman to check the substation, block open the capacitor, and wait for a crew supervisor to call me when he gets in. In the mean time, I'll get my substation manual out and review it before he arrives...

(End of story.)

Mission-critical operations require rested, level-headed people. Not taking this issue seriously will not remedy a potentially serious problem. Communications that make sense take brains that can sort out data and flesh out answers to complex problems whenever they occur.

Instead of only hundreds or a few thousand dollars being placed at risk from a single human operator error, now the costs are in the millions or even billions.[5]

Other data that support the effects of sleep deprivation include:

- The nuclear power plant accident at Three Mile Island took place at 4 a.m. with a crew that had just rotated from day shift to night work.

- The Chernobyl reactor exploded at 1:23 a.m.

- It was shortly after midnight when shift workers at the Bhopal chemical plant began the chain of errors that led to the fatal poisoning of more than 2,000 people.

- The Exxon Valdez oil tanker hit a reef in Alaska that resulted in a devastating oil spill. The time was 12:04 a.m.

- NASA officials had been working 20 hours straight when they made the decision to launch the space shuttle Challenger that sent seven astronauts to their death.

- Is this the end of story? Not likely.

Key Points

- Although he employee may have little to do with the specification, design, or function of his or her work environment, these factors have a lot to do with the quality of that environment, and the security and well-being of the employee.

- A recent survey in Germany revealed that 30–50% of employees complained that supervisors did not take enough time to devote to their subordinates' personal concerns and subsequently, to take appropriate action.

- When employees do not feel secure in their workplace, the foundation of the mission of the workplace is often in jeopardy.

- A feeling of mistrust often clouds the organization that is laying off personnel and consequently, little work can be accomplished.

- Communication is key to the reengineering of a workplace. It can make a difference in employees' morale and well-being, as well as their productivity.

- Mission-critical communications are substantially affected by work climate. It is appropriate to assume that employees are conscious of organizational issues that affect their lives and livelihoods, which this could pose a substantial risk to internal and external operations.

- Many employees have been exposed to a worker who has lost faith in the organization (as it applies to his or her well-being) and have found that the worker has lost touch or has broken communication with his or her superior. It may be that they simply do not get along, but there could be other factors involved that could be remedied if communication played a larger role. In any case, nothing positive will result from the continued rift that exists between them.

- When it comes to reengineering, managers need to ask the right questions, which differ significantly from those that were asked in the past. These questions include: What other ways can we do this? Who needs to be involved? (As opposed to: Who do I want to be involved?) How can I help to protect peoples' interests? Can we control the pace of change, and if so, how do we want to do that?

- Managing in an industry that handles a potentially hazardous substance or product, and seeing problems developing in communications, should lead the manager to act immediately.

- All managers should take ownership of on-going problems that could affect the safety of the operation, its employees, and the people who might be affected by an internal problem.

- Fatigue plays a real part in operations and communications in the workplace.

Discussion Topics

1. Mission-critical communications are substantially affected by work climate. We must assume that employees are conscious of orga-

nizational issues that affect their lives and livelihoods, which could pose a substantial risk to internal and external operations. Discuss the effects of work climate, reengineering, and layoffs. How do they affect communications, and what are some of the successful remedies that you may have read about or experienced?

2. Discuss the effects of shift work in mission-critical work environments. How can an organization help its shift workers cope so that they are not "working zombies" who have the potential to do serious damage?

Speaker: Governor Richard Thornburgh
Location: Three Mile Island nuclear power plant, March 28, 1979

...It fell to us then, to tell the people of central Pennsylvania, as the lieutenant governor did at a 4:30 p.m. press conference, that, "This situation is more complex than the company first led us to believe," that there had indeed been a release of radioactivity into the environment, that the plant might make further discharges, that we were "concerned" about all of this, but that off-site radioactivity levels had been decreasing during the afternoon and there was no evidence, as yet, that they ever had reached the danger point... . We then also began to look elsewhere for sources of information who would be more credible to the public, as well as helpful to us.

Richard Thornburgh, R. (Spring, 1987). "The Three Mile Island Experience: Ten Lessons in Emergency Management," *Industrial Crisis Quarterly*, Vol. 1, Num. 1.

Note: This quote came from an address by Richard Thornburgh, former Governor of Pennsylvania, to the First International Conference on Industrial Crisis Management, New York University, September 5, 1986.

CHAPTER 6

Communications and Decision Making

Importance of Communications in Decision Making

A number of books and articles have appeared in recent years about decision making during emergencies or under crisis conditions. The Federal Emergency Management Agency has developed training for Emergency Program Managers. Some of the world's worst disasters have been scrutinized from a decision-making perspective. Among them are the Valdez oil spill disaster, the Three Mile Island nuclear incident, and the space shuttle *Challenger* disaster. Many readers may be aware of the issues and decisions that led to these disasters. Since their occurrence, decision making has emerged as a field of study in universities and in a number of management training programs worldwide.

One critical element in decision making is communicating information, on which many decisions are based. This chapter will cover a few of the essentials of decision making as they pertain to mission-critical communications. No study on communications used in mission-critical environments would be complete without pointing out the needs of decision makers. Communicators need to be able to give their associates, and managers, and anyone else with whom they come in contact accurate, concise information that will contribute toward rational decision making.

Throughout people's careers they have been exposed to decision making on a personal basis home, and on a professional basis in dealing with problems at work. Some practices have worked, while others have not. Over the years, employees have sifted through these deci-sion-makine practices, keeping some and discarding others.

Many decisions are based on how well informed a person is about a condition or problem. Classifying the knowledge so that it can be used to make a decision is another important part of the process. People have seen what goes on during emergencies on the job, but rarely have they seen what goes on in a real disaster. When people see a disaster on TV, they see what the media wants to show us, which may not accu-rately reflect what is actually going on behind the scenes. One thing that is certain, however, is that some decisions in all our lives will have to be made with uncertain results and, regardless of the results, we will have to communicate with others on our findings.

In the first several hours following a disaster, information may come sporadically. Some of it is accurate information and some is not, but often decisions have to be made based on the information available at a specific time. Because of the major improvements in communica-tions and systems, people may be inundated with information. On the other hand, if communications are down the opposite may be true—We may not have enough information to make a decision with which thay are comfortable. Nonetheless, it may have to be made.

Decision Making and Planning

Sometimes one's decisions are based on observations, such as weather conditions that could affect our operation. Typically, a person moves to an alert status when the weather appears to be threatening the system. In contrast, the person stands down (cancel) the alert status when the storm alters course or dissipates, or does not affect the area for any reason. Then again, the alert status is raised to a higher level if the storm appears threatening.

When a damaging storm arrives, its destructive force is moni-tored as much as possible in protected areas, but there is not much that can be done until the storm has passed and it is safe to survey the dam-age. Then the decision can be made whether it will be necessary to implement recovery procedures or wait for other information to come in before moving ahead with them.

Overextending the work force in the early hours of a disaster can result in inadequate coverage later. Someone must then make a decision on where the new, incoming resources will be used. If the damage is extensive, a decision will have to be made on whether to open remote facilities, which some managers did following the earthquakes in California.

Following the earthquakes, some companies allowed their employees to work out of their homes, using them as temporary offices. They often communicated via cellular phones and modems, some of which were hooked to portable notebook computers, where critical data was exchanged. Knowing that these systems have been used effectively by other companies makes the decision to use them a little easier, but the task still remains of setting them up for use during emergencies. People need to know not only who to call when emergencies are imminent but also where to report when their normal work facility has been damaged or destroyed.

Beneficial Decision-Making Attributes

The *Federal Emergency Management Agency Guide on Decision Making and Problem Solving* covers some of the essential attributes of decision makers. They are being cited in summarized form. The following attributes are part and parcel to the process of decision making:

- Knowledge: What we know about a specific condition or problem.

- Initiative: Assuming personal responsibility for a decision.

- Researching: Work at obtaining information and suspend judgment until the facts are obtained in.

- Advice seeking: Getting input from others.

- Selective data: Seeking pertinent facts.

- Comprehensive view: Look at all available options.

- Currency: Make decisions that respond to current conditions, and take advantage of conditions that presently exist.

- Future orientation: Plan for opportunities that may present themselves in the days ahead.

- Flexibility: Remain open-minded and flexible.

- Creativity: Be open-minded about new concepts, ideas, and approaches.

- Judgment: Decision maker must use good judgment.

- Calculated risk taking: Weigh risks, responsibilities, rewards, and results of alternatives. Then accept consequences, whether positive or negative.

- Self knowledge: Recognize your own capabilities, biases, and limitations. Know where to go for expert information.[1]

Of course, it is important to use these tools advantageously when coming to grips with difficult decisions. Some options will come from other people, which is something that many decision makers often forget. The people on the front lines of the organization are often the best source for good information.

Decision making also involves, setting priorities, which may present problems in a damaging event. Utilities, for example, have to routinely make priorities when storms hit their service area. For example, if a building is located at the end of an electric distribution feeder, with 30 poles down between a facility and a normal power source (in most cases, a distribution substation), it will be necessary to make a decision on whether to put more resources (line repair crews) on that feeder, or put the facility on an alternate undamaged feeder (if one exists). There are a number of options that may be available, but several of them may not be practical or possible.

People expect to get useful information from the electric utility on service restoration progress; however, it may be hours before the utility can get crews on the feeder to begin repairs if many other feeders are damaged. Managers and staff who have responsibility for contacting clients, customers, and other companies, when power outages affect operation will want to get restoration information from the utility as quickly as possible.

However, mission-critical communications for utility management may mean something altogether different than it means to customers. For utilities, customer contact is important, but so is their ability to communicate with their repair crews. Why else would they install multi-million dollar microwave communications systems for this purpose? Of course, utilities do everything possible to maintain communications with the media and customers through conventional means, including radio, and TV, and offices taking telephone calls. Utilities know that they are "lifeline" organizations, responsible for the safety and security of their customers.

Another important aspect of decision making is the way in which problems are communicated to others. thus, communicating decisions to others is an essential part of carrying out a decision, and it weighs in the outcome of the actions people take.

Providing Useful Input in the Decision Making Process

At some point in one's career (hopefully there will be many points), you will be asked for input in the decision-making process. Perhaps you represent a department in an organization that is instrumental in the solution of a problem, or you might be one of the experts in the field that people have come to respect. For whatever reason, other people need your opinion, ideas, or expertise.

Listed below are some key points to consider when the goal is to make a useful contribution to a crucial decision.

- *When asked to attend a meeting for the purpose of provid-*

ing input to a problem, do the research. Always try to come with some ideas listed out on a note card or sheet of paper. When the chairperson asks for brainstorming ideas, you are ready to provide useful input, pulling out the list for reference. If it is known how many people will be invited to the meeting, it may help to make copies of the list to use as handouts. Placing your name and phone extension discreetly at the bottom of the page will make it easy for others to contact you for follow-up information.

- *Speak only when asked for an opinion or an idea.* Others will no doubt have comments, too. Listen for clues that the chairperson may give the group to keep them on track, such as "Let's move on" or "That's a great idea, but it's not within the scope of our problem." In any case, listen for those pointers and take heed.

- *If a great idea occurs to you during the meeting, write it down and keep listening to the discussion.* There may be a better opportunity to present it in the closing minutes of the meeting, or you may want to drop the chairperson a note after the meeting. Explain that the idea was worth some thought and it was necessary to work out some of the issues back at your desk.

- *If the company is in a serious financial bind, it doesn't mean that we should necessarily stay away from ideas that involve spending money.* A brainstorming session for coming up with new ideas would not be served well by limiting them to those that involve no expenditures. The best alternative is to come up with many ideas, including those that require an expenditure. The best idea can then be selected. Some meetings have never gotten off the ground because people kept thinking that their idea would never be approved because it involved an expenditure. Effective managers look at ideas on the basis of solving problems both effectively and efficiently. It may be that an idea has an excellent cost-benefit ratio and is worthy of consideration. One of the first things that a task force needs to know prior to brainstorming is that it has no constraints, money or otherwise. Then people will feel free to share ideas.

- *If it is proper to do so, ask if someone can write ideas on a large notepad for everyone to see.* Everyone likes to see the key ideas developed at the meeting but some people are timid about getting up in front of a group and assisting in this way.

- *Make a summary of key points discussed and date the paper for later reference.* Make a list of people who attended the meeting in case there is a need to follow up with a discussion later. Upon returning to the office, label a clean manila file folder, date it, and keep meeting notes in it for later reference. If it is an ongoing task force, paste or staple a paper calendar on the cover, showing the anticipated meeting dates.

- *Be cautious about discussing some of the information with others outside of the meeting.* Some of the information may be confidential and for committee members only, although the chairperson may not specifically say so.

Effective Communications in Task Force or Committee Work

When involved in task force or committee work, people will be speaking with others in a group atmosphere, often times about sensitive issues that affect others. Mission-critical communicators working in a task force setting will remain focused on the scope and objectives of the task force and do their best to respect other peoples' time.

The opening remarks of a meeting may be general and informal, a way to break the ice. But when the meeting begins in earnest, the language should reflect a serious commitment toward resolving issues. Assignments that are due for the meeting should be handed in or presented in a concise and well researched format. The chairperson should be given undivided attention during the meeting so that it stays on course and on schedule. Employees should avoid personal discussions that distract others. Members of the task force should stay on track, take good notes, and be ready to make a contribution when the time comes to do so. These tips can help make each meeting a profitable experience from the standpoint of communications.

One of the manager's challenges is to be able to recognize when communications are breaking down in a group setting, and take action to get them back on track.

Key Points

- Knowledge is one of the single most important tools of decision making. But decisions must often be made with limited and imprecise information.

- Decisions have to be made with uncertain results, and regardless of the results, we will have to communicate with others on our findings.

- Due to major improvements in communications systems, we may often find ourselves inundated with information, which must be prioritized in order to be useful. During some emergencies the opposite may be true—information may come in sporadically.

- Communications systems must be set up to help the organization deal with disasters. People must know who to call when emergencies are imminent and where they are to report. The plan should include an alternate reporting location in case their normal work facility is damaged.

- Notebook computers and cellular modems can provide an excellent way for employees to communicate with others in the organization, assuming cell sites are operational. Notebook computers were used successfully following the earthquake disasters in California.

- Communications are often affected by interruptions to electric service; however, uninterruptible power supplies and backup generation has made it possible for many organizations to maintain limited services.

Discussion Topics

1. Discuss the relationship between decision making and communications. How can communications be improved to help make decision making simpler for the people making the decisions?

2. Discuss decision-making tactics that work. Focus on someone you know who is good at making decisions and describe his or her methodology. How does he or she make use of information?

3. Discuss how tools or attributes discussed in the chapter can help people become better decision makers and communicators.

4. Describe the communications necessary to ensure a productive meeting.

On computer security...
With the proliferation of client-server technology, the threat of on-line security breaches becomes paramount since more data is stored on personal computers instead of the more protected main frames in the home office...Most people do not know that when information is erased off a disk, it can still be retrieved.

Stacie Berg, Preventing On-Line Break-Ins. (*Gas Daily's NG* June/July, 1995), p. 33.

CHAPTER 7

Using Electronic, PC-Based Systems

Facts, Data, Graphics...and More

There is no denying that electronic systems make a world of difference in our ability to communicate. The Internet makes it possible to communicate with virtually anyone with access to a computer. Some believe that workers are more productive with PCs, while others believe the opposite is true.

Walk into any mall and you will see one or more bookstores stocked to the rafters, and more stores are opening every day. More people are putting out more information—there are more new ideas, opinions, and facts available to anyone who needs them.

Next to the new bookstores in the malls is a new store on the block—the "software superstore." If a person is not feeling up to reading his favorite book in paper form, he can buy a new software "bundle" on compact disc. He may be able to get the book in multimedia form, complete with video clips, sound bites, and interactive hypertext, for about the same price as the hardback in the bookstore, perhaps less.

Computer language seems to be as much a part of our language as the words *notebook, calculator,* and *pen* were a few years ago, and it is rapidly becoming a part of job transaction sets. We are using it to make things happen in the mission-critical environment.

Multimedia Training

Speaking of on the job, how can an employee learn the job faster, learn the language of the job, and get up to speed on the new technology being used in the company? The answer may lie in the computer itself and in the software that drives it, in the form of PC-based training and multimedia.

Multimedia training is the wave of the present. It comes in the form of video, audio, or computer-based training on a wide array of topics. If a person cannot find a particular topic he wants, he can contact a multimedia training and design company, which will develop an individualized custom program. They are as close as the on-line phone directory. CD technology is making everything easier to get to and easier to understand.

Computer simulations and training programs are in use by mission-critical communicators in many areas of industry. There is an excellent chance that your organization is already using them, or that your human resources or training department is aware of them. Since prices are falling, largely due to competition and the technology itself, there is less reluctance for budget-minded departments to get them.

> A popular approach (for multimedia training) is to divide the training into modules, which allows the user to choose the segments he or she needs.... A major issue to consider when using CD-ROM in training is whether the person being trained will have access to the same materials when he or she returns to the regular work environment. In a Local Area Network (LAN) environment, those materials can be provided via the network...multimedia may be the only way to present certain kinds of information.[1]

New Technology Means New Training Challenges

New technology presents a major training problem for large organizations. How are people in the organization getting along with new technology?

Prior to training people to use new technology, it will be necessary to find out what they already know and design a training program based on the survey. Local colleges and universities are rapidly preparing to handle training needs for local industries. Chances are, if they do not already have a program that would be of benefit, they will be happy to design one. Colleges and universities are finding the computer training market quite attractive, and are looking for ways to expand their services to fill those chairs in the evening hours.

Universities are making it possible for students to be a part of campus E-mail and library research system while working from their homes. They routinely take surveys to get a feel for how many students have fax machines, modems, and PCs at home so they can communicate with students more often, and more efficiently, reducing mailing costs in the process.

Many organizations are making computer learning necessary by requiring it for new applicants and by rewriting job descriptions to include it. Because many companies have electronic mail systems, employees must take advantage of the systems to stay up to date on company news and get messages from their colleagues and their manager. Management is pushing the use of paperless systems to communicate. It simply makes good economic sense to do so. However, along with the increased use of electronic mail is the necessity for security. Computer security as an enterprise is growing at an extraordinary rate.

Employees routinely sit down to their PC several times a day and check their E-mail. Mail can be saved, prioritized, forwarded, copied, and redistributed at the touch of a button. Also, technical documentation, can be forwarded to other technicians who work on different shifts. Results of studies made during the day can be kept in a special file for developing and updating reports. There seems to be no limit to the use of electronic documentation for technical and nontechnical applications. A number of applications have been developed to allow people to find their documents quickly by simply remembering a word or phrase that may be in the document, and it makes no difference which word processor was used to write it. The software can read any document created with any popular software package.

Spreadsheet application users can enjoy the same versatility as word processor users through the use of Microsoft Windows™ cross platform file sharing capabilities that allow users to "drag and drop" spreadsheets and graphs into their documents. Presentations that traditionally took weeks to put together a couple of years ago can now be developed in an afternoon. Some high-speed printers are equipped with both Apple Macintosh™ and PC ports to ensure compatibility. Controls and menus are being standardized in software applications, which will reduce the time it takes to master any new application.

Growth of PC Resources in the Mission-Critical Environment

Many mission-critical industries began automating critical services in the same manner. Electro-mechanical devices replaced the manual and purely mechanical ways formerly used to perform specialized tasks. As the computer chip emerged as a method to fine-tune and automate repetitive tasks, it was incorporated into such devices as calculators, controls used in milling steel, protective relays on power systems, and numerous devices used to monitor and control processes. It quickly became clear to many manufacturers that the computer chip could enhance conventional process and control systems, and reduce costs while improving quality.

Supervisory control and data acquisition systems, used in several industries, emerged as circuit boards installed in tall cabinets with large internal fans used for cooling the hot components. Still in its infancy, the desktop computer remained relatively in the background until it gained the respect of engineers and technicians as a reliable tool for completing critical tasks. It remained a tool for performing simple spreadsheet calculations and report writing in the early to late 1980s until it emerged as a proven and versatile tool.

Minicomputers and mainframes ("big iron") were the mainstay of critical applications for industry during the 1970s and much of the 1980s. Then people ever-so-cautiously began to *trust* PCs with more challenging tasks. Many companies began to pilot them for tasks that ran 24 hours a day. The more reliable systems met the challenge without major problems; however, one problem was keeping the power supply stable enough to keep the PCs running. The lucrative business of *power pro-*

tection took off, and uninterruptible power supplies (UPS) devices became standard equipment in offices and in protected areas of industrial complexes.

In the 1990s, many companies have *downsized* critical computer operations to the desktop or deskside, in the case of floor-mounted *tower* units. Multi-chip PCs are now edging out minicomputers and mainframe terminals and workstations, as high performance PCs emerge as valid tools for controlling costs and maintaining production. The cost of hardware is falling and quality is getting better. What is also getting better is diagnostic equipment—hardware and software—to help keep the new systems up and running.

Communications ports enable the PC to link up well with outside data acquisition devices. As equipment in the field or in the plant operates, critical data is fed back to local monitoring points (for example, PCs in control rooms) for review by operators and technical personnel. Equipment in remote locations is "scanned" every few seconds and numbers are updated on the screen following each scan. Operators are rapidly growing skilled at monitoring systems and processes on PC screens, and they are often being consulted during the design and specification phases of new systems development.

The ability to visualize processes is better than ever before through the use of high-resolution computer graphics, which are rapidly replacing character-based software programs that were not very adept at modeling or providing realistic images. The user interface of choice is the graphical user interface (GUI), which provides a standard *platform* for new applications. The monitors that are being specified for new systems provide crystal-clear images that make the operator's job more pleasant and less tiring than with the older low-resolution screens. The number of available colors has gone from sixteen to nearly infinity, enabling software designers to shade and provide contrast in ways that enhance visualization and operation. Since graphics accelerators (special PC circuit boards) post images on the screens quickly, there is little concern these days for using images that are memory intensive when software applications are being written.

From the operator's perspective, PCs can be simpler to use than minicomputer based SCADA systems, and faulty equipment can be changed out quickly and easily, so the operator does not have to wait for long periods without a replacement system. The new systems are less proprietary than before, when some problems required a technician from the factory to get the system up and running. End user applications software is specified and designed using rapid applications development (RAD) software that has grown more powerful, making it possible to develop sophisticated applications in record time, using fewer programmers. Standard communications protocols make it possible for cross-platform information sharing.

Productive Use of PC Technology and Related Devices

PC devices and systems are communications tools. Of course, some people would say that PCs are here for amusement. But in both applications, they are being used as communications tools, whether for game playing, simulation, or data acquisition. In a real sense, when a person plays a game on a computer, she is looking for amusement through digital communication with the game programmer. What did he plant behind the next corner? When she sees it, what should she do? How many points will she get if she does it right? Will the game (programmer) give her enough points to go on to the next level?

Used in the mission-critical environment, the PC becomes a tool to help people interact with other people, devices, and systems. Employees depend on the software to "understand" and be intuitive in order to meet their needs, although they cannot really speak with it in conventional, spontaneous ways, as they can with other people. At least, not yet. That may be the "brass ring" that many computer scientists are reaching for as new systems are designed. *Organizations need computers that work well with humans rather than humans that must work harder to learn to work with computers.*

If the same line of thinking is used for systems as was used for procedures in the discussion on transaction sets, one will likely come to the conclusion that systems must be precise. They must mirror the technical needs of users and allow them to not only operate systems distant from their location, but also give the operators the needed flexibility to play "what if," to help them prepare for potential emergencies. New systems are employing both the operating and training aspects and needs of operators, so that the PC will become the versatile on-time/off-time tool of choice. There are more software applications that are job oriented as opposed to task oriented, allowing the user to do some training, including the observing of simulations on-line by setting up simulations or by reviewing technical information.

The packages may offer integrated tools to process, record, view, log, listen, and transact without switching to other stand alone applications. If each subprogram is designed well, the operator is more likely to adopt the entire package as the tool of choice. Of course, if one or two parts of the application are marginal in utility, then the operator may look for one that meets his needs more effectively. How many times has software been abandoned due to its cumbersome handling of an important task? If users look on shelves in their offices, they will find software that was not used because it simply was not worth the effort to learn it or use it, or was quickly made obsolete by a competitor. This is a clear indication that software designers must work in step with users if their product is to be accepted in a given industry. Competition is growing fierce as new software development tools are bringing in more small companies that can meet the user's needs better, cheaper, and faster.

Microsoft Corporation launched Windows 95,™ a PC operating system, in August 1995. Advertising suggested that it could put out to pasture the tired disc operating system (DOS) and earlier versions of Windows software. However, as with earlier versions,Windows 95 had to go through the same criteria for robustness before it met with the hard-earned respect of users. People met with some initial installation problems which were dealt with by the "help desk" personnel.

A manufacturer of software can tell its potential customers that its new software will be stable and will open up new opportunities, but if the company launches the product and people have major installation problems, two things are bound to happen: 1) The company will face an angry crowd that has spent hours installing and configuring a faulty product; and 2) they will pay less attention to the pre-launch hype in the future. Software manufacturers will also force the customer's hand in purchasing a competitive product. People do not have the time to spend hours installing software, and they will be further put off by poor documentation. When a customer is installing software and a message flashes on the screen similar to the following: *'Invalid VxD dynamic link call from IOS(03)+00000B5D to device "page file", service 7'*, he is likely to get frustrated in a hurry. Microsoft Windows changed many peoples' lives for the better and remains an excellent tool for the PC user. While it has some drawbacks, it enjoys a loyal following both in industry and in the home PC market.

If there is one thing that the reader should come away with after reading this chapter, is that people have a low tolerance for faulty systems and cryptic language that mean nothing to anyone outside of a manufacturer's organization. Applying this notion to control systems alarms, one will find that operators have even less tolerance for cryptic language because they are often constrained even more by time. They must be able to recognize an alarm condition on sight and act upon it immediately. Operators must also be able to diagnose a group of alarms, which may offer a more complete picture as to what has occurred prior to dispatching a technician. So in the design of alarm indicators, electronic or electro-mechanical, singular as well as group alarm signaling methods must be considered, as well as how operators will react to them.

No one should be overly critical of one industry, because all industries are guilty at one time or another of letting cryptic communications go outside of their organization. But it should be emphasized that in the future there will be less tolerance for it by consumers. With the information age has come a tremendous respect for *time*. Everyone is sensitive to how much time a product or system costs.

Operator's/User's Role in Software and Hardware Development

What is the operator's responsibility during development? Perhaps it is to be more involved with development than she has been in the past. The operator must not only be involved, but also she must be interested in developing a better tool. Frequently, operators look at software development as an activity that they should avoid, largely because they may think that it involves skills foreign to them. They may associate design with coding the software and not with the many other activities that go on behind the scenes. For this reason, the project manager should make the various development tasks clear to task force members, especially when they have little or no background in software or hardware technology. In most companies, the "glass walls" surrounding information systems have fallen. Programmers are camping out with users, which is the more successful approach to software development.

On the hardware side, operators need to remain in high-profile roles in specification and development. Loose fits and poor color coding, and knee-banging, back-straining consoles must be a thing of the past. There is no excuse today for perpetuating poor design. Operators need to know how they can facilitate change, which is one of the critical roles of the project manager: to get operators into the design/development picture and keep them there.

Project managers sometimes believe that operators add significantly to development costs by requesting nonstandard hardware design. They may, therefore, fail to get operator input, or only include it in small or less significant segments of a project. This method serves to perpetuate poor design and leads to problems in using the final product. It is also clearly out of date, since most manufacturers want to please the end user and mitigate problems associated with faulty hardware design. In addition it also points up dysfunctional communications in the design, development, manufacture and marketing track that virtually all products must take. A more positive and profitable approach involves the operator/user in all segments of product design. It is clear that operator input can help reduce the more costly effects of negligent or problematic design in critical systems, which can lead to damaging and costly events.

Key Points

- Multimedia training is one of the most rapidly growing fields in the information age.

- Computer simulations and PC-based training programs are used by many organizations.

- New technology means new training challenges. Local colleges and universities are listening to industry and developing programs to meet training needs.

- E-mail offers flexibility for updating others on current issues.

- The personal computer emerged as a reliable tool during the 1980's, worthy of a broad base of mission-critical applications.

- Client-server technology emerged as the option for workgroup PC applications and information sharing in the 1990s.

- Computer graphics grew quickly in the early 1990s. The user interface of choice became the graphical user interface (GUI) which provided a standard software *platform* for new applications.

- From the operator's perspective, PC-based systems are often attractive alternatives to larger systems.

- Systems are employing both the operating and training needs of operators. Operators may develop simulations to play "what if" to help them prepare for emergency conditions.

- Operators must be able to quickly recognize alarms and groups of alarms, and be able to act on the information immediately. Designers of alarms and support communications must take this need into consideration and deliver the right package to the client.

- There will be less tolerance for cryptic alarms and errors in software installation as time pressures increase.

- Operator input must remain in the forefront of software and hardware design, and throughout the development process.

Discussion Topics

1.   Discuss the use of personal computers in the mission-critical work environment. Is productivity suffering in any area as the result of PC use? What areas in the organization have benefited from the use of PCs?

2.   Discuss the use of electronic mail and its impact on communications.

3.   What are some methods that managers can use to monitor PC use and to help ensure that they are used as intended?

4.   Discuss the training going on in the organization to benefit computer users. What impact has it had on operations?

Between the brain's concept processing systems and those that generate words and sentences lie the mediation systems (we propose). Evidence for this neural brokerage is beginning to emerge. ...Mediation systems not only select the correct words to express a particular concept, but they also direct the generation of sentence structures that express relations among concepts. ...When a person speaks, these systems govern those responsible for word formation and syntax; when a person understands speech, the word formation systems drive the mediation systems.

Damasio, A.R. and Damasio, H. (September, 1992). "Brain and Language. " *Scientific American*, p. 93.

CHAPTER 8

Systems in Use in Organizations

Use of Systems in Transaction Set (T-Set) Communications

This chapter will provide an overview of considerations for devices and systems that foster effective T-Set communications. T-Set communications were previously defined as any communications that are appropriate for maintaining or advancing the organization in its mission, and minimizing risk as tasks are completed. They include T-Sets used by mission-critical communicators and those that would be considered appropriate for inclusion in job or task T-Sets should they be developed in the future. All communications that employ the job T-Set, and hence, the task T-Set language used for completing tasks in the MCCs environment should be considered mission-critical communications for the organization. As people engage in transactions, they often use systems and devices as a medium for communicating T-Set language.

This chapter will briefly discuss some devices that are used in the workplace for communicating, collecting data, monitoring, and other functions that are considered to be part and parcel to this study. This is not an attempt to dissuade the organization from considering devices and systems that are currently available in the marketplace. And because new systems are being introduced every day, this chapter will not dwell on the merits of any given system. This chapter simply offers suggestions for evaluating some of the critical concerns of the users of such systems. Although there is an entire industry and a science that deal with ergonomics and human factors design, this chapter will not tread deeply into these areas, except as they relate to communication, and only then will present some ideas for those who are interested in enhancing their use of systems.

Use of advanced electronic communications systems is a routine part of today's environment. If an employee is not using a telephone, she is using a fax, a cell phone, a beeper, or perhaps E-mail. Face-to-face communications seem to be growing more infrequent, except for time spent in meetings, and even then, teleconferencing is often employed.

Also in use are advanced microwave systems and 800 mHz and 900 mHz simulcast radio systems. People have grown accustomed to telling others to "reach me on E-mail," or to "page" or "beep" me. Character-based symbols are used to communicate happiness, sadness, hatred, and love on the Internet. Employees can now develop colorful presentations using graphics programs on the PC, and then send them on diskette or CD to a colleague at a distant location. Managers routinely schedule sessions on commercial on-line services, such as America Online™ and CompuServe™.

Security has also become an issue, with many firms installing safeguards to limit employee access to outside PC on-line services, for fear of them giving away company secrets and details of new processes, or contracting computer viruses, which are a growing threat to all computer users.

In addition, industries employ advanced computer systems to retrieve data, such as supervisory control and data acquisition (SCADA), GIS (Geographic Information Systems), and AM/FM (Automated Mapping and Facilities Management) systems to correlate hardware and plant resources with geographic information. Utilities routinely map their service territories and overlay equipment, including electric facilities, gas pipelines, switch locations, and telecommunications facilities, along with the locations of remote supply facilities and tie points. Even the number of units of a specific device are installed in a given geographic area can be ascertained with these systems by overlaying a database with seamless geographic information.

Utilities regularly control power system switching and bring remote generators online using energy management systems. Rail transportation centers can also perform similar operations from remote locations. The number of applications and variety of hardware being contemplated, designed, and prototyped for industries almost seems endless. The market for such devices and systems remains vigilant, looking for new ways to do more with fewer resources, cutting transaction costs to the bone. There is nothing wrong with this practice if it does not compromise the primary goal of being certain that mission-critical communications are not impeded.

Who will be chosen to use the advanced systems?

The demand for people who are proficient communicators continues to increase. Pick up a Sunday paper from a large city and read the "Help Wanted" section. The jobs industry is promulgating in record numbers positions that are associated with information, and the proliferation and sharing of it. Information sharing postions (computer network administrators, network engineers, client server programmers, and database designers), advertising and print publication specialists (desktop publishers, designers, editors, and writers), telecommunications project (engineers, project managers, technicians), and associated positions are on the rise. The hackneyed position requirement, "must be a good communicator," remains in the ads because there is an endless demand for people who can communicate well, regardless of the task. In contrast, people who cannot communicate well are left to find positions in which precise and effective communication is a secondary need. And, that list is growing shorter. In fact one has to struggle a bit these days to find jobs in which communications are not a major factor.

Managers must consider who among their employees are not only effective *organizational communicators*, but are also *task-precise communicators*. One could say that effective organizational communicators are high-performance communicators in a wide range of applications, but they may not be task-precise communicators, that is, those who are effective in specialized areas of organizations. The organizational communicator is, however, valuable to the organization in a wide variety of settings, such as overseeing the delivery of messages to the public concerning company operations, or facilitating productive meetings, conferences, or seminars.

Task-precise communicators, on the other hand, may follow more closely the transaction set language that was previously explored in earlier chapters of this book. It is possible to have an organizational communicator who is also an effective task-precise communicator, largely due to his or her close involvement with front-line, mission-critical operations. It is more common to find a task-precise communicator who may not have the necessary experience to communicate for the organization, but may perform very well as a mission-critical communicator in a select area of the operation.

Once a manager finds the individual she is looking for, either on the street or within the organization, he or she must work with the internal systems, which may or may not promote effective communication and task completion.

The Role of Transaction Costs in Mission-Critical Systems

Industries consider economics in every project, including those that are mission-critical. Classic *make vs. buy* decisions are made every day in industry. Cost-benefit studies and feasibility studies often consider the cost associated with *transactions*, which are defined in this segment as specific operations that, when grouped with other transactions may comprise a complete process. The simplest example is a list of alarms that come in to a central facility to indicate a breach in security, such as occurs if an intruder were to make his way into a secure building, first tripping a perimeter alarm, then a window or door alarm, and finally an alarm on a door internal to the building. Another example is the investment in a telecommunications system in an industry that has an existing high-volume transaction load for data and voice communications. The company will look at lease arrangements on existing towers versus the purchase and siting of new, privately-owned towers.

Every process that demands some type of transaction is a candidate for the consideration of transaction costs, including those that may not be readily apparent. As managers reduce transaction costs, however, they must keep a watchful eye on the cost of communications as they relate to and are instrumental in completing transactions.

Transaction costs, like production costs, have many components, such as:

- the cost of placing an order,

- the costs of monitoring performance and ensuring that contractors do not shirk their responsibilities in terms of effort or quality, and

- the costs of maintaining sufficient safety stock to prevent coordination problems caused by reliance upon outside suppliers.

Transaction costs economics (TCE) argues that the structure of firms and industries at a given time is chosen to minimize total costs, and represents a balance between production costs associated with producing goods or services and transaction costs associated with coordinating and arranging for production.[1]

If one compares this notion with the study of mission-critical systems, some readers may find it difficult to make the connection between TCE and highly specialized systems used in mission-critical operations, but ultimately, some of the same evaluations and decisions must be made, regardless of the industry. One might argue that there is a point at which the organization must abandon the notion of transaction cost if it in any way impairs safety or adds in any way to risk, especially where human life is at stake. However, effective project or strategic planning managers do not abandon TCE in their studies, rather they acknowledge it for what it is and make recommendations accordingly.

Some costs must be borne by the organization, even if they appear on the surface to be unreasonable. If this were not the case, advanced systems used in medicine, for example, would never make it off the drawing board. Although hospitals elect to outsource many of their tests, they nevertheless maintain the same types of technical equipment as do the firms that specialize outside of the hospital or medical center. Patients expect the hospital to maintain a certain amount of research and diagnostic equipment, even though the tests they conduct can escalate medical costs beyond what the patient can pay, with or without the aid of insurance.

When specifying process control equipment, industries can choose from dozens of suppliers worldwide; however, only a few may be capable of delivering the mix of features and price that industries can afford. During processing, these systems may deliver the equivalent of transactions, but in ways that are foreign to the production environment. Typically, the cost of transactions is not a consideration when, for example, supervisory control and data acquisition or energy management systems (EMS) are being considered, because utilities (a primary user) process numerous transactions—switch operations, readings, alarms, generator functions, etc.—during the course of a day. The transaction costs of an energy management system, for example, would be minuscule over the life of the system, compared to the transaction cost of a magnetic resonance imaging (MRI) machine at a medical center. Comparing the two would not be an effective measure, although both systems are critical to the organizations that invest in them, are in the mainstream of mission-critical operations and MCCs, and process information relative to a critical function going on at the facility.

Managers would nonetheless look at investing in the technology in terms of cost-benefit, but the EMS cost-benefit would fall under a number of categories including reliability, economic operation, and its capabilities to facilitate power system interchange and control. Thus the MRI would be looked at from the standpoint of patient safety, revenue generated per use, its reliability and safety to the operator, and other factors of importance to the physician or medical organization.

In addition to its fundamental operation as a device that performs a task, the equipment should be able to simplify the tasks of gathering, reading, and interpreting data.

System Needs of the Mission-Critical Communicator

Managers must be careful when criticizing the systems put in place by a project team. People typically put a lot of thought, research, and study into specifying a system that will be used by a department or group of individuals for a number of years. They can take criticism about how a part of the system malfunctions, but a manager has to employ tact when giving feedback to a project manager or team since feelings can get hurt. Most managers have probably heard people talking about a glitch in a computer system, or a problem with a conveyor belt or other device on an assembly line. These glitches crop up with some of the best systems and must be addressed.

What is difficult to overlook is when the same type of problems occur when a new system is installed. When the engineering and design do not include quite enough research, experience, feedback, or testing, the same types of problems often reappear in new devices and systems, only to be ridiculed and cursed by users repeatedly. But, this is the nature of the quality improvement process: to incorporate what is learned back into the design process for future versions of a device or system.

For instance, a person visited an appliance store looking for a new dishwasher armed to the teeth with tidbits of information about dishwashers that he had used before. He began opening doors, looking for the placement of the silverware basket; the operation of the hinges on the door; the fit and finish of the dish, pots, and pans tray; and the design of the lower and upper spray arms that shoot water over the dishes.

Then it hits him. Even the more expensive models employ some of the same troublesome features that he had seen before: loose-fitting parts, detergent cups that do not latch well or look like they will stick closed, hinges and metal fittings that will rust in a short while, poorly labeled controls, undersized motors and poorly fitting insulation around the tub. He is frustrated, but he needs a new dishwasher, so he takes a chance and buys the one that looks like it will hold up a little better. He wishes that he could be there when the engineers design the new models, but of course he cannot.

Then the man goes to work and sees the same kinds of problems on the new computer control systems that a project team is considering—problems that were either never uncovered by the engineers or that remain too cost prohibitive to address by the manufacturer. The fictional study that follows will help the reader form a better picture of the way this study of systems parallels the study of mission-critical communications.

A utility is considering the installation of a new control center and support systems. The control center is a room in which system operators dispatch technicians to problem locations on the system. In summary, the system operators, or dispatchers, monitor power system parameters, such as system voltage, transmission line loading (the amount of power being transmitted over a given high-voltage line), the output of generators, and the flow of power to and from neighboring power systems. They also perform a number of other mission-critical tasks in the center. In order to do this, they use powerful computers that are linked via communications facilities to substations and generating stations throughout their service territory. A reference was made to this type of system earlier in the text.

From time to time, utilities replace outmoded computers and related equipment, such as meters and printers. When this occurs, a project team may be appointed to research the new systems that are available and then make recommendations to people who approve contracts for the installation of the new equipment. As with the simple dishwasher example, there are traps and troublesome characteristics that must be avoided if at all possible. What occurs, however, is that the project team must make the best possible recommendations that the budget allows, in the time allowed for project completion. While some system operators are strategically placed on the project team, there are bound to be problems that mirror those that arose with the old system. Although the hope is that advancements in the technology will make the new system superior to the one being replaced, often new problems occur or old ones are carried over into the new system by an inexperienced or unsuspecting design team.

Some of these problems will affect the communications that go on between users, and also between users and the technicians they communicate with at remote locations. Other problems will not be uncovered until the system has been in use for months or even years. They will lie dormant until a user uncovers them, hopefully without serious incident.

Assume that a small research team is charged with contributing to a formal report on the operation of a new control center facility, including its energy management system, the metering, the consoles, and the auxiliary devices, all of which have been installed for one year. They are charged with interviewing the operators to gather information. The report will then be used to help the company avoid pitfalls when specifying control center equipment in future installations. It will be important for the team to uncover things gone right as well as things gone wrong at the facility.

At the end of the interviews, a report is delivered to the team leader on items of concern to operators. For example, the list might include the following items that have a bearing on how information is processed in the center:

1. Telephone console buttons that are depressed to answer a call sometimes do not "latch" when pushed in, and the calling party is sometimes disconnected.

2. Operators often have to leave their console to research items away from their desks. When calls come in to the various consoles and operators are not at their stations there is no clear way to determine whose console is ringing, so all operators must return to their consoles to check. (Note: there are five consoles situated several feet apart in the center.)

3. Meters that include strip (paper) chart recorders are sometimes difficult to read because the inking pen is located over the top of the bend made by the roller in the chart mechanism, making a portion of the chart out of the line of sight of the operator. The operator must then leave her chair and stand on tiptoes or a stool to read the most recent information on the chart over the top of the roller. (See Figure 8-1.)

4. The operator must move away from the telephone and CRT display to retrieve substation and other paper-based diagrams. (Cabinets that hold diagrams should be located closer to the operator.)

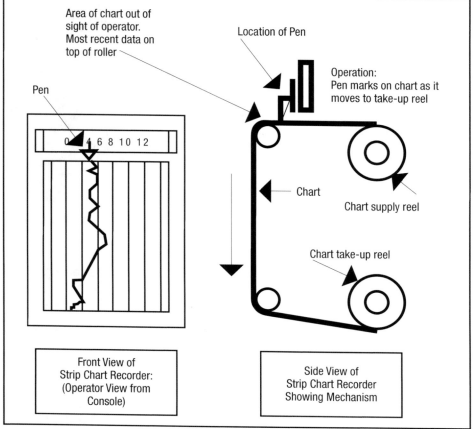

Figure 8-1: Chart Recorder Diagram

5. Alarms are not color coded properly. When a specific event occurs on the system, many alarms come up on the CRT as high-priority alarms, yet several of them are not of the same level of priority and importance as others.

6. The system map board, a board stationed in front of the operators that contains a diagram that mimics their high-voltage transmission system, is too dark in color, and it is difficult to pick out the substation locations from across the room. Due to this problem operators note that it can be diffi-

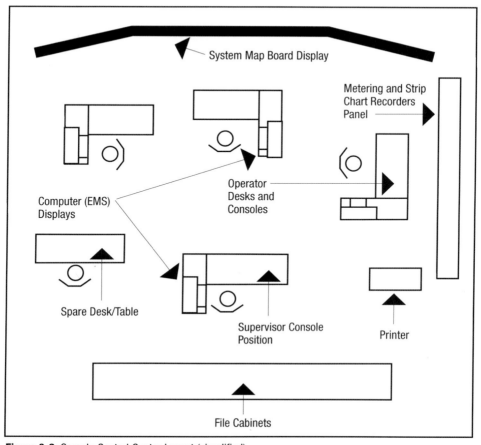

Figure 8-2: Sample Control Center Layout (simplified)

cult to track work in progress and unusual system conditions on the board.

7. Operators assert that the noise level in the room is often too high for conducting conversations on the phone. Background noise can interfere with conversations going on between the operators and the technicians doing the troubleshooting at substations, which could lead to switching errors and problems related to poor communications. (See Figure 8-2.)

8. The new telecommunications system, which includes an 800-mHz radio and backbone microwave system, has zones in which communication drops out while operators are transmitting. This affects communications between the control center and vehicles, and between vehicles and the operations buildings located throughout the service area. Some technicians have been forced to carry cell phones in addition to radios in order to backup radio communications.

9. The energy management system software is proprietary, and a direct hardware interface between the EMS computer and the company mainframe computer is not possible. Special applications must be developed to enable the mainframe to share information with the energy management system computer, adding to development, installation, and training costs, as well as to maintenance costs.

10. The location of the restroom facilities at the control center necessitates that the operator spend more time away from his desk, which puts a burden on the other operators in the center who are already handling more transactions than in the past. It also forces the people who are calling in from the field to wait longer to transact business, because the principal operator is the only person familiar with the work going on in his area. Since the men's restroom has only one commode, when it is occupied, the operator must return to his desk and wait or he must use another restroom far removed from the center, exacerbating the problem. In addition, management has refused a request to install additional facilities to remedy the problem.

The previous example is representative of the types of problems that companies have with systems and devices that directly affect communications and work flow, of which many are mission-critical. So, where does the organization stand with respect to these kinds of issues? Upon closer inspection, one can see that each issue has merit and has not been simply trumped up by a disgruntled operator.

A more thorough look at the design of similar centers prior to specification and fabrication might have uncovered some of these problems, but others might not have been uncovered until the operators actually spent time at their position. How do managers avoid making the same kinds of mistakes in design and specification? Although there are really no quick answers to this question, one thing that managers can do is listen and then fix these problems as soon as possible. Be aware when visiting centers (or any existing facilities) for study purposes that the people who work in the facilities can give a "tourist version" of their thoughts and ideas about the facility or they can be truly candid. Imagine how many design errors could potentially be carried over into new products. It happens more than we would like to believe.

Key Points

- As we engage in transactions with others on the job, we use systems and devices as a means for communicating.

- There are critical concerns for the design of systems. For example supervisory control and data acquisition systems, used in a number of industries, must be designed to match growing client needs.

- People who use advanced systems must be excellent communicators, both as organizational communicators and task-precise communicators, each with talents for handling specific types of communications.

- The role of transaction costs was explored in TCE analysis. It is sometimes difficult to compare transaction costs with other industries and come up with cost-benefit numbers that have useful meaning for some systems.

- Whatever the equipment, it should have qualities that make it simple to gather, read, and interpret data, in addition to its other principal uses.

- It is difficult to overlook design flaws that have plagued specific types of equipment for many years.

- Without user intervention, design errors are carried over to new products.

Discussion Topics

1. Discuss the use of pagers in the workplace. Have they made a positive impact on mission-critical communications? Are they used by too many people, or should everyone have one in the organization? Discuss the same issues for cellular phones.

2. How has security been affected by the use of advanced communications devices?

3. The book discusses the organizational communicator and the task-precise communicator. Describe the role of the organizational communicator during emergencies.

4. Describe the use of alarms in mission-critical applications in your organization and how they are handled. What has been done to make alarms more meaningful to computer users?

5. Discuss some of the installation problems that were experienced with a system at your facility. How did communications fit into the installation picture? Were there problems that were related to communications?

If individual computers are powerful, consider the network–the linking of separate units into a whole that's greater than the sum of the parts. The ultimate computer network, of course, is the Internet–a series of software programs that allow computers any-where in the world to exchange, via telephone or data transmis-sion lines, information with each other quickly, reliably, and cheaply. Companies providing access to and navigation tools for the Net offer compelling investment opportunities.

Laderman, J.M., and Smith, G. (August 28, 1995). "Investing in High Tech," *Business Week*, p.53.

CHAPTER 9

Communications and Contingency Planning

Written Communications

There are a number of books on the market that cover written communications more thoroughly than will be covered here. Many guides cover general writing methods for all types of writing. This chapter will cover writing *procedures, accurate logs, recording telephone transactions, and similar writing*, in a mission-critical environment. Look for a narrow focus on written communications in this chapter that may be added to your existing communications tools. The goal is to offer a concise blend of *mission-critical* writing methods for the reader's consideration. If the methods are used in earnest, they are effective.

Written communications are all around us, in both the routine work environment and in the high-tension "control center" environment to which some of us have been exposed. In such films as The China Syndrome and War Games, movie goers took their places as bystanders, learning more about the ramifications of the negative side of technology in no uncertain terms. The films were based on reality and were underscored by such events as the the Chernobyl and Three Mile Island incidents. High-impact, gut-wrenching events in industry are not fantasy, rather they are very real. They *can* happen, although many people who are associated with them have been known to downplay their significance and loss potential.

What often occurs, however, is that news conferences are provided, information is disseminated to the media, a postmortem report or a series of them are written, and the "lessons learned" appear in targeted publications where they may or may not be read. Many people learned from these events that information—or the lack of it, or the manipulation of it—can greatly affect the appropriate outcome: the implementation of remedial action and installation of improved systems.

Considerable research is done at the university level, often uncovering underlying problems that may not have been discovered by "official" investigators. For example, Dr. Mark Maier of the University of New York undertook a comprehensive study on the Challenger disaster, which made available to others a substantial amount of information on that event. He put together a complete research kit on the study, composed of several videos and support documents.

From the standpoint of mission-critical communications as they relate to high-impact events, what issues demand attention?

Writing Contingency Plans

There is no importance in the bottom line, or in any phase of the operation of any industry *if there are no workable contingency plans installed in the organization*. Contingency, emergency, or business continuity plans, as they are often called today, are far more important than any single marketing, finance, new product development, strategic, or other plan found in any organization. They are what sets the truly competitive, societal, worldly, and mission-conscious organization apart from its competitors.

Without a workable emergency plan that explains the recovery or restoration of the core services of an organization, the organization is truly built on a crises-encumbered foundation. Contingency plans *must be* integral to their work and the training of people in the organization. There can be no exceptions to this rule in the mission-critical organization, nor in any other organization. As it has been said by many a seasoned manager with more than one crisis behind them, the penalty for not following this recommendation is too painful to imagine. When a crisis comes, it catches the unwary organization flat-footed, without the simplest of resources to mount a recovery effort. Losses are often too staggering to imagine, often in the millions and, occasionally, in the billions of dollars. Costs tend to escalate for each day a disaster is out of control.

Managers often fail to realize that their operations are not islands in and out of themselves. When something damaging happens to a company facility, it can often have an effect on the homes and businesses in close proximity. It not only affects service to customers who depend upon the product or service for their operation, but also affects the employees and the vendors who help to keep the facility in operation.

Contingency plans are documented strategies and procedures that guide people through a series of steps to mitigate the consequences of a damaging event. The term is used generically in this book to describe any plans that deal with preparedness, response, and restoration of damaged or interrupted core systems or services. Organizations must have contingency plans and test them regularly or they stand a good chance of losing everything when disaster strikes.

Some of the key reasons for having contingency plans are the following reasons:

- To restore mission-critical systems and services as safely and quickly as possible to a specified level of operation. (As you read further, think about what these systems and services are and list them for later review as potential areas to cover with plans.)

- To mitigate further damage through incorrect remedial action.

- To eliminate unsafe conditions and plan methods to handle injuries, if they occur.

- To reduce recovery costs.

- To provide an orderly, well-coordinated, proven approach to handle a damaging event.

- To help reduce the number of decisions that must be made during recovery.

- To restore revenue-producing systems in order to reduce the likelihood of financial hardship.

- To maintain customer/stakeholder confidence and the financial health of the organization.

A few of the many questions that readers may have about contingency planning include:

1. Do I need a lot of formal classroom training to help my organization become better prepared?

2. How much of my time might be required to get my organization on track with appropriate plans?

3. Will my organization be able to handle a disaster as effectively aslarger organizations that have more resources?

4. What do other organizations expect from us when disaster strikes?

The answer to the first question about the need formal classroom training is no. A modular approach is suggested, breaking the project down into subprojects that can be completed by team members. It is similar to using a training manual that covers several departments or a more complex topic. The only prerequisite for success in developing contingency plans, along with good communications and coordination skills, is a desire to see the organization be more prepared for damaging events. If technical skills are needed, they can be secured by calling someone in the organization, such as an industry expert, or even a faculty member at a local university.

Although the reader will be given information in this book to help improve contingency plan writing skills, many organizations have at least one person who is good at writing procedures without a lot of assistance. That person may want to be involved in this project. The task of actually writing the plan can be delegated near the end of the project, if desired.

Notes will suffice to begin the process and can be given to the person who will do the word processing. Anyone can be involved with the final editing after the procedures are on paper. Charts and graphics can be completed by the media, graphics, or public relations department.

The answer to the second question on how much time might be required may be a surprise to many readers. Contingency planning may require only an hour or two a week for each planning group member in the early stages of the project. The time each member spends may grow shorter as the plan reaches its final production stages. If an individual is doing this work full time, then he or she will still need to meet with others, which will take a little time. Once the plan is installed, the only time that will be required will be for revisions, upgrades, and maintenance to the plan; to train people on the use of the plan; and to take some time each year to test the plan. Of course, time requirements will vary by the type of plan, the interest in moving forward to get it in place, and the number of people involved with the project.

Chances are, the time required for the planning will be less than for most other projects in the organization, and the pay back can be significantly greater in terms of the security of the organization and of minimizing the loss or interruption to core operations. These are the solid benefits of staying on the road to become a better planned organization. If management is focused on becoming better prepared, there will be more momentum. Readers are urged to think about their future involvement in contingency planning.

The answer to the third question about the ability of a small organization to handle a disaster as competently as larger organizations may also be of interest. The fact is, the number of resources that an organization has is only one factor in the formula for recovery. The more appropriate question might be, How will the organization be able to use valuable resources to its advantage without a good plan?

Resources mean very little without the knowledge of how to deploy them in the most effective way. An organization could have billions of dollars tied up in materials and equipment, and still be totally ineffective in dealing with an emergency. Therefore, a smaller organization with a good plan may outperform a larger organization in handling a crisis.

The final question, What do other organizations expect from my organization when disaster strikes?, is very important because the answer entails two of the most important factors in crisis planning: coordination and support. An organization may not have all of the resources necessary to handle a major emergency. In fact, if it did I would be surprised. Organizations rarely have all that they need, but prepared organizations know where to obtain resources.

For example, a similar organization located in a nearby city may also be short of some resources, but may be able to lend something if they knew others needed it. Is it possible for you to support each other in time of need? Is it possible to have a "mutual assistance" plan cover a major loss? Such a plan and agreement may be a critical factor in your organization's survival.

Drafting a mutual assistance plan may be one of the most important parts of developing a company-wide contingency plan. It simply makes sense to share resources when disaster strikes. A good example of this can be found in utilities, where mutual assistance is practiced whenever a utility experiences a natural disaster that destroys facilities in the field. Electric utilities, for example, may belong to a mutual assistance pact that allows them to share resources, including line crews, trucks and materials across state lines. For example, out-of-state utility crews were used extensively during the major hurricanes and earthquakes, for example, helping utilities restore service to millions of people as quickly as possible. Financial organizations, such as major banks, often make arrangements to do off site processing for the loss of computer facilities.

In summary, getting involved with contingency planning is critical because:

- Organizations that are more prepared for emergencies are better able to cope with the administrative, technical, logistical, and personal problems that surface.

- Organizations that do not have preparedness and response plans will likely find it difficult to deal with these problems, and may therefore jeopardize the safety of employees and the operation of the organization.

- Recovery will likely cost organizations much more than if they had the right plans installed.

- It can take several days before help arrives. A plan can help make the organization self-sufficient until others are able to assist with the recovery. As a general rule, self-sufficiency should be planned for the first 72 hours or longer following a damaging event. After a few days, some help may be available. It is also important to check with our vendors to see if our emergency plans can be coordinated.

It can happen to any organization! Today, tomorrow, or next year—at some point an event will threaten the operation. Disasters and emergencies of all levels of severity happen to some of the best managed organizations in the world, and they can happen at any time. Organizations often experience emergencies on a Friday night, or early Saturday or Sunday morning, when it is difficult to get people on the phone, let alone get them involved in recovery. Leaders in many of the finest organizations often say that if they had had better plans to deal with emergencies they could have done a much better job.

Organizations that are prepared did not become that way overnight, and they did not get there by wishing they could successfully confront the difficult issues. Crisis-prepared organizations are aggressively improving their chances for the next major threat on a regular basis.

The action item that follows could easily be the most important statement in this book:

> Any organization, regardless of size, must have a viable contingency plan in place to cover the loss of core services should disaster strike. That plan should be tested, at minimum, annually, with follow-up reports that include action items to be assigned to appropriate individuals for disposition. Mission-critical writing includes the development of the plan and reports and training materials involving the use of the plan.

No organization, regardless of its resources or talent, will have everything worked out in advance for every event, nor will it have fool-proof plans. But everything we know today about contingency planning tells us that having a plan is the best way to minimize the risk of total loss. The low-probability, high-impact event is the one that can take us out of the picture forever. It is important to think about what would happen to the most critical services during a damaging event and then *plan for that event.*

The real fear for the experienced manager is confronting an emergency or disaster head on and then realizing that no tested contingency plans are available. There are many questions and very few answers. There is nothing worked out with vendors, contractors, employees, other departments, or other company facilities. The list goes on. What do we do now?

Assume that your organization is ready to begin in earnest to develop a good contingency plan. For example, when you begin to develop contingency plans for computer resources recovery, (one of the more common starting points in industry), the thought processes are similar to those you can use elsewhere in the organization. Do not make the assumption that you need to go about the work in a totally different way. The following is a list of important considerations for developing contingency or emergency plans in any environment:

1. Narrow the scope of a contingency plan to increase clarity. Writing one all-inclusive plan to cover several types of emergencies might be the reason that plans intimidate intended users. (They may not want to pick up the plan let alone read it!) For example, information services or telecommunications plans should deal with recovery of those services, and not several others. Quality, not quantity, is important in developing emergency plans.

2. Make procedures concise. If you have four or five different steps or procedures buried in one paragraph, it is easy to see how one or two might be lost in the rush to complete them. Keep procedures short and easy to digest. Use outlines or bulleted lists of procedures for maximum impact.

3. Pay attention to how the plan is organized. Think of a plan as a tool for working toward a result step by step. If there is usually lead time to prepare, be it long or short, use it to your advantage. For example, such would be the case in a natural disaster plan, when there may be hours to prepare for an oncoming storm. Put some checklists in the front of the plan to get the company organized in a hurry.

4. Keep building and refining plans. Encourage various operations and support departments to develop emergency plans that will help them recover their core services. This could be as simple as a department developing a plan to deal with the temporary loss of a mainframe computer, or as complex as a facilities department relocating the headquarters for the loss of a building. Once a plan is installed, make sure it is tested and refined to meet user needs.

5. Keep outside agencies and vendors tuned-in to plans. Determine how the plans affect people outside. This includes vendors; emergency management community— officials, police, rescue teams; and others who may have to assist. Use brochures and ads to keep the public informed.

6. Hold regular tests. Corporate-level emergency and disaster recovery plans should be tested at least once a year. This requires that people get involved, from officer level to entry level. Since employees become valuable resources when disaster strikes, so get them on board with the training and testing as soon as possible.

7. Brief new managers and supervisors. Any new supervisor orientation program should include a briefing about emergency planning and emergency operations. Since employees sometimes ask their supervisor what they are expected to do during emergencies, so it is important for the supervisor to know how the answer. Knowledge of emergency plan-

ning helps the supervisor understand how the company will respond, so that he or she may offer the services of the department under crisis conditions. The supervisor may also be more likely to begin to formulate departmental emergency plans after a briefing.

8. Establish leadership early. Managers, supervisors, and staff need to know who is in charge from the outset of recovery operations. Plans must identify the person or persons in charge, and establish a clear line of communication. This will help eliminate some of the idle time that can be experienced while people are awaiting answers to questions that must be posed to upper management in the organization.

9. Make contingency plans simple to revise. A plan that requires a lot of approvals for revision, or is otherwise difficult to revise, will not be revised often. Keep the planning and approvals process simple. Give the planner the authority to make improvements and revisions without a lot of red tape. Hopefully, when a planner or planners are assigned to write or revise a plan, there will be enough confidence in them to allow them to do their job.

10. Resolve action items. Action items, which are generated from tests, should be addressed on a high-priority basis. If it is known that there will be a problem in a given area if a specific emergency occurs, then it can be made less costly and time consuming by addressing the issue before the emergency occurs.

11. Test standby generator and uninterruptible power supply systems regularly. If you plan to occupy a specific site that has back-up power, make sure back-up capacity is sufficient. The best test is a real test. Instead of operating the generator as simply a test, drop the normal supply to a facility and see what is covered by the backup power system and what is not. Make sure outlets are clearly marked, and

that occupants know what they can and cannot use. Also determine how long the organization will be able to operate on standby system with existing fuel.

12. Test the assumptions of decision makers. When you hold emergency exercises, try to ferret out assumptions that have been made by decision makers. Those untested assumptions could lead you to higher recovery costs and a longer recovery. Get assumptions on paper and test them along with methods for recovery.

A good way to begin contingency planning is to call a meeting with colleagues to discuss areas of vulnerability and narrow the focus to systems that are critical to an operation—that is, systems you cannot do without even forseveral hours or a day. Then look at the following steps to get the plan developed as quickly as possible:

1. Once core services are identified, look at events that might put them out of action.

2. Once out of action, what strategies will be used to restore them?

3. Turn the strategies into procedures, and identify the people in the organization who will be responsible for completing them.

4. Write the plan using a straightforward, logical approach. Keep it simple.

5. Make sure everyone is aware of the plan and his or role to restore services.

6. Test the plan.

7. Write a report citing weak areas, strong areas, and areas in need of immediate and longer term attention.

8. Assign the action items.

9. Make sure action items are addressed; revisit them at quarterly meetings.

10. Hold another test.

11. Continue improving the plan.

12. Do not rest until people in the organization take the emergency plan seriously and know their roles.

Writing Technical Procedures and Plans

An introduction to contingency plan writing was given in the previous section, and is representative of writing that is focused on a specific process. This section will cover some of the mechanics of writing for mission-critical communicators.

It is safe to say that mission-critical communicators do not often need a long-winded approach to written information. They need a brief, accurate, and modular approach from writers. Several important characteristics of mission-critical writing include the following:

- Readers want the writer to understand their time constraints for reading and comprehending written information.

- If a diagram can make a process easier to understand it should be considered for use in the document.

- Readers enjoy reading short paragraphs that do not contain a lot of procedures that need to be weeded out of the paragraph and prioritized before they can be used.

- Keep procedures in concise bulleted lists, numbered lists, or in outline format.

Use a clear, easy-to-read font in all documentation. Some people are more receptive to a serif font while others like a San serif font. My preference for procedural documentation is a sans style font. In the True Type (Windows™) fonts, for example, you may want to give Arial font at 11 or 12 points in size a try. It is a very clean-looking font that reproduces well after several trips to the copier.

- When writing procedures, do not tell the user what you do not want him or her to do. Instead, keep the user directed toward what you want done. For Example:

Wrong: If the #2 Feeder Ammeter doesn't read under 6.0 Amps, don't open switch A.

Better: When the #2 Feeder Ammeter reads less than 6.0 Amps, open switch A.

Best:
___1.   Read #2 Feeder Ammeter.
___2.   Record the time and the present ammeter reading.
___3.   Wait until ammeter reading is less than 6.0 Amps.
___4.   When ammeter reading is less than 6.0 Amps, open Switch 'A'.
___5.   Check Switch A open.
___6.   Place a numbered Yellow Tag on Switch A Control Handle.
___7.   Record the time that you opened Switch A .

- Complete a thought or procedure without writing about something else that may distract the reader.

- Writing should be patterned after job and task transaction sets, if they exist for the person performing the task.

Writing Useful and Accurate Logs

Logs can be thought of as one of the most important types of written communications that are kept in the mission-critical organization. Some practitioners, however, find them difficult to maintain, especially in the early stages of learning a job. New employees often need coaching in accurate log keeping, and even veterans sometimes forget what information should and shouldn't go into a log.

The basics of log keeping are not difficult, but they do demand some attention. However, attention is often what mission-critical communicators find in short supply while on shift; when the shift is over, the log is often continued by the relief operator, who may not find it convenient to take the time to correct errors or better organize the log after the shift.

For example assume that the log is in paper form, as it is in many locations. (Electronic logs will be discussed shortly.) Further, assume it is a written log for an operator (used here generically for an individual who communicates with field technicians on the telephone or radio.) Such a log may include brief remarks concerning the following topics (some may be more appropriate than others in specific jobs) :

- With whom is the operator speaking?

- Is he alone or with others?

- Where is the person located?

- What circumstances brought him to the location?

- Is there a pending emergency or existing emergency condition?

- Did he do anything before he called the operator?

- What is he doing now at the location?

- Is it appropriate for him to be at that location?

- What is the purpose of him calling the operator?

- Does he require assistance from the operator?

- Are there any problems that require attention by others?

- What will he be doing prior to leaving the location?

- What time is he leaving the location?

- Will he be required to call the operator again prior to leaving?

- When he leaves, will there be any conditions left abnormal?

- If yes, will tags or other designation be left to indicate that the abnormal condition exists?

These observations can be extremely important if a problem exists at the location, because they will be key to reconstructing an event for a report. More importantly, they may help the organization avoid a problem in the future.

The operator working in the plant control room, air traffic controller, dispatcher, technician must often work in a hostile environment. As soon as their pen comes down on the paper to write a log entry another phone rings, another alarm sounds, a line printer chatters away in the distance, or other distractions are present. These are the conditions in which the operator must function, but the log must be written, and written well.

Administratively, what can be done to help the operator keep his or her log so that it is a useful tool? Perhaps the following questions will be of value:

- Can the logbook form be changed to help make the process of logging information easier?

- Can check boxes be added to allow the operator to check off strings of information that are repetitive in nature? For example, if weather information or temperatures were required, could a visual tool be printed on the form to allow the operator/technician to circle or check off a given condition? It is easier to make a mark than it is to write something out.

- Can the form be color coded in some way to make information easier to distinguish?

- Is it faster and easier to write with a felt-tip pen than a ball point or a pencil?

- Can some generic information be pre-printed on the log form to save time?

- Can the operator take his or her log away from the facility at the end of the shift to polish it up and perhaps fax it ito a central location for assembly into a daily report?

These are just a few ideas to get the improvement process underway. If the issue of logs is a painful one for the person writing the log or reading it, then perhaps it is time to take a closer look at improving the process.

Electronic Logs

The idea of keeping electronic logs would have been impractical for many people not long ago. Today, however, electronic or computerized log entry is a very real alternative that can offer decided advantages over handwritten logs. For example, any information that could be automatically generated by a computer, such as writing in a date, weather conditions, or other programmed information, would save the operator time in log creation. In newer applications, such as those that offer graphical user interface (GUI) forms on a screen, the addition of check boxes, "radio" buttons, slide bars, and virtual switches or buttons that can be pre-programmed to perform specific tasks for the operator could help with record keeping.

The introduction of personal digital assistants (PDAs) has opened up logging information and uploading it to a computer a realistic alternative for many people. PDAs with handwriting recognition are used daily worldwide and can offer many companies a fast way to compile daily reports and logs from field technicians, operators, service engineers, or others. Many PDAs are equipped with modems that make it possible to file an electronic log from virtually any location.

Electronic logging via a smart device, whether portable or stationary, offers real time savings over conventional logging and should therefore be explored for application in more mission-critical areas of operation. As PDAs are refined and as their prices continue to plummet, they will be a more attractive alternative. This would be especially true if handwritten logs had to be later transcribed to develop a report. With electronic logs, files can be merged and scanned for errors in minutes or seconds, and more easily archived for later use. Hard copies are always an option if they are ever needed.

Telephone Transactions

Some of the pitfalls of telephone communications have already been explored which lie outside of the job or task T-Set in earlier chapters. When we deal with others over the phone, they do not have the ability to see what is going on at their location and thus miss a large part of the communications picture. Everyone must try to overcome this disadvantage by being more effective communicators: what we say, how we say it, and what we demand of the person on the other end of the phone. When one senses that something is wrong, he must often take steps to regain control that may have lost through an emotional response on either end of the phone. Perhaps there will be a time when the person with whom you are speaking is in danger or perhaps an expensive piece of equipment is in jeopardy unless immediate action is taken to remedy the situation.

There have been many occasions when a technician has been in a remote location and something has gone wrong there. Perhaps the only way to report the condition is on a telephone or radio. This is common in the utility industry, when relay or substation technicians are performing routine tests and a wrong circuit gets shorted out.

In the control center, the system operator may suddenly see a group of alarms come in from the substation and he or she knows that a technician is performing maintenance or testing at the substation. It is evident that something has gone wrong which may or may not be the fault of the technician. If the error is serious enough the entire control building at the substation may be filled with toxic smoke or fumes, in a matter of a few minutes, making it impossible for the technician to immediately remedy the situation. The technician may not be able to call into the control center to report the mishap, except by radio or cell phone.

Once on the phone, a fact-finding mission may be difficult to conduct, especially if the technician is shaken or deeply disturbed by the incident. Some of the most competent field technical people can be so shaken by such events that someone else may have to be called in to examine the facility and file a verbal report on the damage. Similar situations can be expected in other industries and other professions.

The training programs that are developed for people in mission-critical, high-risk technical jobs must take into account these scenarios, because it is reasonable to believe that they will grow more common in the future. Telephone communications training should therefore include the following points:

- Operator briefing on what can go wrong in specific locations where telephone use is expected.

- Use of proper transaction set language for given tasks.

- Instructions on how to speak on the telephone so that the user can be understood, even under difficult conditions.

- When not to use the telephone (while performing specific tasks).

- Reporting telephone problems.

- Using the telephone during emergency conditions, and when communications must be kept concise to free up the phone for other use.

- Where specific numbers are kept to communicate with other facilities.

- Appropriate use of cell phones, pagers, portable fax machines, modems; and sending data as well as conducting voice communications.

Key Points

- Contingency plans are necessary and important to the survival of any organization, especially those engaged in mission-critical services.

- The issues surrounding emergency or contingency plan development are explored. Contingency planning requires few resources and little time, but it does involve regular revision, training, and testing.

- Resources can mean very little without planning for their use during emergencies.

- Readers are urged to consider their involvement in the planning process. Emergency planning requires a "champion" of the need for contingency plans to make sure that the minimum requirements are in place and people are trained to respond.

- Organizations are urged to develop relationships with other organizations that could provide assistance if disaster strikes.

- Contingency plans should be tested (at a minimum) annually.

- Useful tips to help the organization develop the best plan include the necessity of narrowing the scope of the plan, making procedures concise, using good plan organization methods, refining plans on a continual basis, talking with other organizations about plans, and holding tests to ferret out needs.

- Readers want writers to understand their needs. Procedures should be written according to those needs.

- Accurate writing and formatting of procedures and logs can be very important. Log forms can help the operator maintain quality if they are designed well.

- Training should address telephone use in mission-critical jobs.

Discussion Topics

1. What contingency plans are needed in your organization? Do they exist?

2. How can contingency plans be developed in critical areas of the organization? Who might be involved? How can they be developed in the least possible time? If you are not employed, consider talking with someone you know who works in a mission-critical job. Is she aware of plans and her involvement in them?

3. Discuss the use of contingency plans in recent emergencies or disasters. Consider creating a file of clippings of news articles that relate to how organizations recovered from damaging events. What were some of the important "lessons learned"?

4. How are computer resources recovered following a disaster at your work location? What plans are in place to perform work in a back-up mode, such as handling forms and information without computer resources?

Telepower—the union of telecommunications and information technologies to create change—is today the number one force of change in modern society. It is more powerful than oil, or great wealth or even petty tyranny. The reason this is true is the simple reality of change and political upheaval in the world of the past five years...these are all directly and intimately tied to Telepower.

Pelton, J.N., Ph.D. (1992).*Future View: Communications, Technology and Society in the 21st Century*, Boulder, CO. 1992, p. ix.

Author's note: Joseph N. Pelton is director of the oldest graduate telecommunications program in the United States, which is located at the University of Colorado at Boulder, as well as director of the university based Future Center: The Center for Advanced Research in Telecommunications.

CHAPTER 10

Using Visual Tools for Training and Operations

Where Do We Use Diagrams and Visuals?

Using diagrams when communicating ideas can be very effective. This chapter will introduce some of the ways in which diagrams can be used effectively throughout the organization in mission-critical applications, as well as in promotional opportunities.

Diagrams, or "visuals", as many people call them, can make or break a presentation. However, presenters often limit their scope in the use of diagrams. Many readers have, no doubt, been to presentations that were boring because the presenter did not use visuals, or used visuals that were crude, colorless, or poorly drawn. On the flip side, many readers have probably attended presentations that were outstanding because the presenter used a broad spectrum of visuals that were colorful and well designed. He or she may have used them to advertise a new product, diagram a change in the organization structure, or show how a process has changed to make it less costly or to improve quality.

Diagrams are used extensively in workbooks, handouts, brochures, manuals, proposals, and reports. Many software applications, including word processors and spreadsheets that are introduced in the organization contain tools to help the user draw charts and simple illustrations to enhance documents. Flowcharts are used by programmers to help them understand how an application will perform. Managers use organization charts to help them understand how their company is staffed and who is in charge of a given department or section. Diagrams are also used in transportation, chemical industries, research organizations, and in the utilities to help introduce new information. More people are catching on to the advantages of using diagrams in virtually all correspondence, report writing, and in operating or procedure manuals.

Developing Effective Diagrams

This section will cover some of the basics of diagram development. Some of the issues that we might consider when deciding to use diagrams include:

- Will the diagram help make a new procedure or process easier for the user to understand?

- Will a diagram help simplify a complex process?

- Can the diagram fit on one page, or will several pages be required?

- Can color be used in the diagram to help users visually isolate specific processes?

- Can standard symbols be used—for example, those used in flowcharting?

- Will the diagram require the services of an expert designer in order to draw it effectively or can it be done with off-the-shelf software by a novice?

- Would adding several diagrams contribute significantly to the expense of the document?

- Will the document be simple to reproduce or will special reproduction equipment be needed to properly duplicate the diagrams?

- What information will have to be written inside of the diagram? Will it fit inside of the symbols?

- Will the process flow from left to right on the page, top to bottom, or in some other fashion?

- If charts are to be included, what types will be effective in displaying the data?

- Will the user expect to see diagrams in the document or primarily text, or a balance of both?

Such questions should be reviewed during the document planning stage, but many of them will be simple to answer or may not present a problem with the application.

Diagrams can help to expedite the transfer of information because people tend to think in a nonlinear fashion. There are several visual-based training programs available today for people who want to learn more about creating documents that are easy to read and use in everyday work.

Robert E. Horn's Mapping Hypertext[1] offers amazing insight on how symbols and blocks can be used to help display information that might otherwise be difficult to understand. Many of Horn's ideas have helped organizations effectively organize and present critical information in a manner that promotes retention.[2]

Another approach to developing ideas is to use a Mind Map™ and the process of Mind Mapping, which makes use of diagrams instead of written outlines to document information. Mind Mapping can offer nearly anyone an effective way to develop information as well as display it.

When Mind Mapping is used, the central idea or topic is written inside of a box or other symbol in the center of a sheet of paper. The person constructing the map (whom we will call a mapper) then draws lines that radiate out from the center topic. On those lines the mapper writes subtopics that apply to the main topic, similar to main branches radiating out from the trunk of a tree. Subtopics often give rise to ideas that relate to those topics. These ideas or thoughts are then written on smaller "branches" that radiate out from the main branches. When the mind mapper is finished he or she has a diagram that conveys an entire thought process which can then be used to construct something else, perhaps a resolution to a problem, or a new device or process.[3]

Using Software to Create Visual or Graphics-Based Information

Using software to create diagrams is probably the most practical way to do the job given today's outstanding PC-based applications. Some advantages of using software are:

- The user can immediately see how a diagram will look before it is printed.

- Objects (symbols) can be electronically pasted on a diagram and easily moved or deleted as needed.

- Lines connecting symbols can be drawn quickly and easily with precision, using only a pointing device such as a mouse or trackball.

- Electronic "grid lines" make it simple to align objects on the screen and ensure that they are aligned in the finished product.

- Symbols can be "grouped" or "ungrouped" so that the user can manipulate them easily on the diagram.

- There is less of a need for artistic talent since diagram symbols are already drawn for the user.

- Text in the diagram symbols can be edited, resized, and duplicated with ease.

- The entire diagram can be electronically "cut and pasted" into other applications, such as documents or spreadsheets.

- At least one application offers the capability of automatically drawing a diagram by using a simple script language.

Numerous other advantages are offered by the large variety of charting and graphics software available for the PC or Macintosh™ compatible computers. The reader may want to view the sample diagrams created with software at the end of this chapter (See Figures 10-1–10-4).

Step-By-Step Diagram Development: A Model

This section will review a process for developing an effective visual for inclusion in a sample document. This model is representative of what can be done; however, it is a simplification of a process and is certainly not the only method available for doing the work. The reader is urged to take these steps into consideration when the time comes to develop documentation that involves the use of diagrams:

1. Try one of the software packages on the market, whether it works with a PC or Macintosh operating system. Both are excellent for the task and neither offers a decided advantage over the other.

2. Once the software is on the computer and is available, practice with it for a while to get used to using the principal features.

3. If the software offers several alternatives to the style of the diagram, take this into consideration for the project.

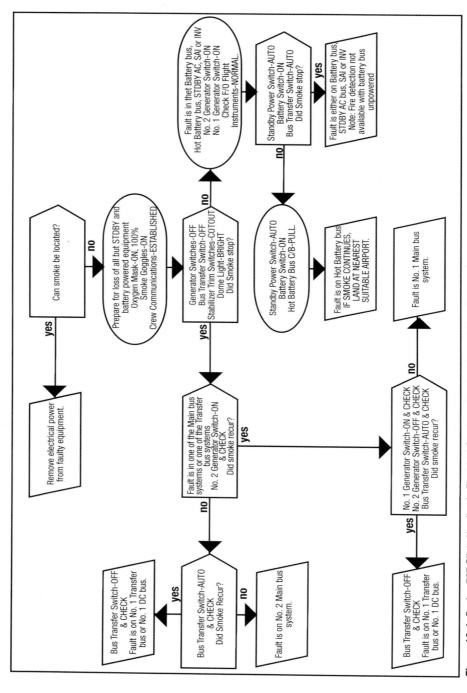

Figure 10-1: Boeing 737 Pilots Handbook: Electrical Smoke or Fire (courtesy of Clear Software)

BOEING 737 Pilot's Handbook : Electrical Smoke or Fire

{*HIDE !}
Can smoke be located?
    (yes)
    Remove electrical power from faulty equipment.!
    (no)
    Prepare for loss of all but STDBY and battery powered
    equipment: | Oxygen Mask-ON, 100% |
    Smoke Goggles-ON |
    Crew Communications-ESTABLISHED.
    Generator Switches-OFF |
    Bus Transfer Switch-OFF |
    Stabilizer Trim Switches-COTOUT |
    Dome Light-BRIGHT |
    Did Smoke stop?
        (yes)
        Fault is in one of the Main bus systems or one of the Transfer bus systems |
        No.2 Generator Switch-ON & CHECK |
        Did Smoke Recur?
            (yes)
            No.1 Generator Switch-ON & CHECK |
            No.2 Generator Switch-OFF & CHECK |
            Bus Transfer Switch-AUTO & CHECK |
            Did Smoke Recur?
                (yes)
                Bus Transfer Switch-OFF & CHECK |
                Fault is on No.1 Transfer bus | or No.1 DC bus.!
                (no)
                Fault is on No.1 Main bus system.!
        (no)
        Bus Transfer Switch-AUTO & CHECK |
        Did Smoke Recur?
            (no)
            Fault is on No.2 Main bus system.!
            (yes)
            Bus Transfer Switch-OFF & CHECK |
            Fault is on No.1 Transfer bus | or No.1 DC bus.!
    (no)
    Fault is in the Battery bus, |
    Hot Battery bus, STDBY AC, SAI or INV |
    No.2 Generator Switch-ON |
    No.1 Generator Switch-ON |
    Check F/O Flight Instruments-NORMAL.
    Standby Power Switch-AUTO |
    Battery Switch-ON |
    Bus Transfer Switch-AUTO. |
    Did smoke stop?
        (yes)
        Fault is either on Battery bus, | STDBY AC bus , SAI or INV |
        Note: Fire detection not available with battery bus unpowered.
        (no)
        Standby Power Switch-AUTO |
        Battery Switch-ON |
        Hot Battery Bus C/B-PULL.
        Fault is on Hot Battery bus |
        IF SMOKE CONTINUES, LAND AT NEAREST SUITABLE AIRPORT.

Figure 10-2: Script for Boeing 737 Diagram (courtesy of Clear Software)

OLE Overview

CorelFLOW supports Object Linking and Embedding both as a server and client. As a server, CorelFLOW supplies data to other Windows applications. As a client, CorelFLOW receives data from other Windows applications.

Embedding as a Server: CorelFLOW, the server supplies data to another Windows application, the client. The data is stored in the other application, and therefore can only be accessed from that client file. Any updating to embedded objects must be initiated in the client application.

Embedding as a Client: CorelFLOW, the client, receives data from another Windows application, the server. The data is stored in CorelFLOW and therefore is accessed by the single CorelFLOW file. Updates to the embedded objects must be initiated in CorelFLOW.

Linking as a Server: CorelFLOW, the server, supplies data to another Windows application, the client. The data is stored in CorelFLOW; therefore the data can be accessed by several different files or applications. When the CorelFLOW data is updated, all linked files are updated.

Linking as a Client: CorelFLOW, the client, receives data from another Windows application, the server. The data is stored within the other application and the CorelFLOW diagram may be one of many files accessing the source data. When the data is updated in the other application, the CorelFLOW file is updated.

| OLE Contents | Contents | Linking as a Client |

Figure 10-3: OLE Overview (courtesy of Clear Software)

4. If the user does not have an immediate project he or she may want to work through a tutorial that can be supplied with the product, or simply select a task that is done every day in the workplace and create a diagram to replicate the process.

5. It is important to realize that no one is an immediate expert at creating diagrams. As with any other task, the user will get better at it with practice.

6. If the software permits the user to "script" the process in outline form, it may be simpler to write an outline or script of the process from which the diagram will be constructed later.

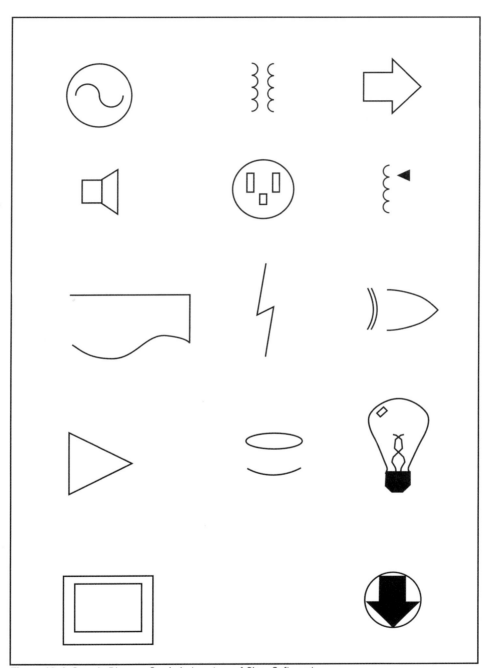

Figure 10-4: Sample Diagram Symbols (courtesy of Clear Software)

7. If the software is solely a drawing tool, simply begin placing symbols on the electronic documents as if you were "assembling" the task, one procedure at a time.

8. Place an appropriate symbol on the screen and write in a step. The user may want to number the steps as he or she writes them in the symbol, or wait until the entire diagram is complete and consider numbering at that time.

9. If you are not sure which symbols to use, simply use a box to hold the text, resizing the box if the text is more than what the symbol will hold.

10. As the symbols are dropped onto the electronic page, they are connected with arrows to show relationships to one another. Some programs allow the user to move boxes around on the page and the software will automatically adjust the arrows and maintain a reasonably consistent shape. If the lines and arrows begin to look disorganized, it may be time to consider placement of the symbols to correct the positions of the lines.

11. Diagram building is a repetitive process, placing boxes and other symbols on the screen. If a standard size is contemplated for all boxes or symbols, the user can save some time by copying symbols to the clipboard and repetitively pasting them on the screen. Once placed, the user can then connect the symbols with lines and arrow symbols.

12. Once the diagram is reasonably complete, decide whether any formatting changes would be appropriate, such as headers, footers, titles, colors, margins, and page orientation.

13. It may also be appropriate to adjust border width on boxes, or line width and arrow width on the connecting lines.

14. If the software allows, decide whether the chart can fit on a single page by selecting "fit on one page" from the print menu. In this case, the software will automatically scale the diagram to fit or it will tell you that the diagram may be too large to fit on one page. If the diagram must fit on one page, the user will want to resize all of the boxes to accommodate the fit.

15. A draft of the diagram can then be printed and inspected. If colors were used, the printer may take a little more time to print the diagram. If grayscale was used instead of color to fill the boxes, this can also increase print time.

16. If you need to "export" the diagram to another application, appropriate look on the File menu to see if exporting the diagram is allowed. If not, it may be possible to copy all of the information to the clipboard and simply paste it into the application (such as a word processor), which may also be running in the background. Most Windows-based word processors allow these options.

17. Experiment with the software and try new ways of creating diagrams when time allows. You can create a "library" of diagrams that can then be printed in the future to speed the development process.

Key Points

- Diagrams are useful in many types of written communications and can help improve understanding.

- Graphics-based software makes it possible for novice users to create useful, attractive diagrams.

- The usefulness of Mind Mapping and other systems for communicating thoughts can be useful in the organization.

- Software diagramming tools can offer important advantages.

Discussion Topics

1. Discuss the use of diagrams and visuals in various types of documentation, including reports, memos, letters, proposals, annual reports, procedure manuals, employee manuals, safety manuals, and technical manuals.

2. Discuss the common concerns that many people have about using visuals. Are visuals needed in all types of documentation that involve descriptions of processes?

3. Put yourself in the position of the user of a procedure manual. What would you like to see illustrated? Would you like to see color used in diagrams? What disadvantages are introduced with the use of color in visuals? Hint: Background colors can sometimes interfere with text colors in the blocks of a diagram. Think of some other problems.

4. How is software used in your organization to develop visuals for various projects? Does everyone have access to software that may be used for creating good visuals? Have training needs been addressed?

5. If you are a frequent airline traveler, consider looking at the emergency procedures brochure located in the seat pocket. How are diagrams used to explain emergency devices on the aircraft? Are they clear and simple to follow? How could they be improved?

On the importance of written communication...

This letter is written to insure that management is fully aware of the seriousness of the current O-Ring erosion problem in the SRM joints from an engineering standpoint... . It is my honest and very real fear that if we do not take immediate action to dedicate a team to solve the problem, with the field joint having the number one priority, then we stand in jeopardy of losing a flight along with all the launch pad facilities.

Roger M. Boisjoly, Engineer, Morton Thiokol (solid rocket booster manufacturer)
(Source listed below in Author's Note)

Author's Note: This is an excerpt from a memo written by Mr. Boisjoly July 31, 1985 in a letter written to a superior on the safety aspects of space shuttle rocked boosters prior to the Challenger disaster. The memo is from the exhibits offered by Mark Maier, Ph.D. in his work "A Major Malfunction..." The Story Behind the Space Shuttle Challenger Disaster, Vol. II, Summary Chronology, Exhibits & Figures, Copyright 1992, The Research Foundation of the State University of New York.

CHAPTER 11

Overview of Expert Systems Used in Mission-Critical Communications Environments

What are Expert Systems?

In recent years, computer programming has included the writing of code for highly specialized, dynamic, and interactive applications. Programs called expert systems — the result of setting down to computer code the knowledge of a human expert in a given field — are now in use in a variety of applications around the world. Such programs can be made integral to the decision making processes for critical and non-critical tasks. Expert systems are being used in utilities for applications that are both fundamental and critical to system operation.

An overview of some of the expert systems in use in utilities will be followed by an analysis of the collective use of these systems in critical areas of utility operation. Their strengths and weaknesses will also be examined. The objective of this study is not to dispute the value of expert systems, since their use has already shown remarkable benefits. However, the author believes that it is important for users to fully understand the implications of expert system use in mission-critical applications, as they apply to communications and system operation.

Development Software

This section contains a brief description of the trends in application development, which will help define some of the terms that will be used throughout the chapter and provide a generic description of how expert systems can be used. However, the reader is urged to consult other sources for a more complete study of terms and programming procedures.

Application programming in expert systems traditionally requires an in-depth knowledge of coding in the language of choice, be it PROLOG, LISP, C, or other language. Expert system programs of significant size can take months, perhaps years, to successfully develop. To meet the needs of industries that want faster application development, software manufacturers have created development programs sometimes called *expert system shells*, because they consist of a convenient development "shell" or interface that is user friendly. They are also called "development environments" by some vendors. These prototyping packages are effectively decreasing development time, making it possible for *knowledge engineers* — people who play a major role in developing the actual programs — to concentrate more on the content of the application than on the tedious mechanics of writing code. To be accepted for use, expert systems must offer viable alternatives and must be cost-effective.

Expert systems applications development software can be used in conjunction with many standard operating systems and user interfaces, such as DOS (IBM, Digital Research, and Microsoft, for example), Microsoft Windows, and IBM OS/2.[1] Some products offer the capability to compile the finished program into a stand-alone application that can be transported to virtually any other platform in an organization. For example, a knowledge engineer can develop an expert system on his or her PC, compile the code into an *executable* program — one that is ready to run — and then hand the program to a power plant operator or engineer to install on a PC in the power plant. *Run-time* modules are also available that allow end-users to run a program that cannot be compiled without having to buy the entire application development software in order to run the program.

Expert systems can be written to run on mainframe, minicomputer, and microcomputer hardware, which allows maximum flexibility for the end-user. Hardware technology advancements have allowed companies to develop powerful programs that run on inexpensive personal computers, which reduces the financial commitment necessary to get a company up and running with expert system software. This has put expert systems within reach of many organizations. Where performance has overshadowed the issue of cost, expert systems have found their way to higher performance minicomputers, and to the mainframe systems that are common in many utilities.

Expert systems can be found in real-time applications, where electronic communications links between sensors and computers allow the monitoring of critical processes and plant operating systems. Parameters such as temperature, pressure, voltage, and water level are continually monitored by the computer, and alarms can be triggered to summon a human operator to intervene when a reading goes out of programmed limits. The expert system (software and hardware) can also be used to initiate a sequence of events to control a monitored device or system, or it can be used to *recommend* an appropriate action. Programmed with the heuristics (rules-of-thumb) of an experienced worker, an expert system can also be used as a tool to help train the inexperienced technician or operator.

To further illustrate how an expert system works, suppose that data coming from an electric generator show the temperature of a critical component to be 300° F. The knowledge base contains information indicating that this component's normal temperature is 250° F. One of the rules encoded in the *inference engine*, the component of an expert system that determines the rules to use to find an acceptable solution, might be: *If component temperature exceeds normal by 50° F, then sound the alarm.* Once this rule is executed, the user interface would alert the operator and might provide the message saying that "There is a 64% probability that the hydrogen cooler is blocked, suggest checking the cooler before shutting down the unit."

This same problem could be solved by using conventional computer programming techniques, but the expert-systems approach has three advantages. First, artificial intelligence (AI) programming languages make it easier to encode "If...then" rules, reducing programming time. Second, because the inference engine and the knowledge base — consisting of expert knowledge: in the form of heuristics, facts, and rules — have been separated, new rules and facts can be incorporated without having to completely reprogram, as might be the case with conventional programming. Finally, with expert systems, the process of problem solving is mainly probabilistic and intuitive, an approach well adapted for complex problems with many uncertainties.[2]

As a final note, the terms *AI* and *expert systems* are used interchangeably in this chapter. This is to say that expert systems are a branch of study under artificial intelligence, which can include such fields as robotics, neural networks, and other areas that attempt to simulate human intelligence through computer programming. Although, the focus of this chapter is in the area of expert systems, there is also significant activity in the area of neural networks and robotics in electric utility research. With these general facts in mind, the next section will discuss why utilities use expert systems, and will look at some real applications.

The Lure of Expert Systems in Utility Operation

A program manager for AI at a large corporation was quoted as saying he gets back $15 for every dollar spent on AI. Claims like this have enticed utility managers, programmers, and engineers to give AI a hard look in a number of applications. Electric utility operation is based on economics, with the goal being the low-cost energy producer of choice. To operate a competitive electric utility is to produce and sell electric power at a cost per kilowatt-hour that is both reasonable and relatively stable. Over the long haul, this has been the case; however, customer demand has forced utilities to take measures that have forced up rates, and in so doing, has brought on competition from commercial nonutility generators. The capital intensive utility must continually strive to be at least as competitive as its neighboring producer, or risk being bought out by another utility or going bankrupt. Thus, the lure of cost-saving alternatives is a very real part of utility operation.

Many expert systems are developed for existing applications. They are offered as alternatives or ways to complement traditional methods of monitoring systems and making decisions related to a specific problem or task. AI systems are not, in general, promoted as programs that are superior to humans, but rather as complementary to humans. However, the Buck Rogers in many of us often shows through when the eager consultant or programmer describes what can be done with them. The wary user, however, must be able to separate fact from fiction, and know what he or she is really purchasing at the outset. The cost of the software is often of little significance compared to the time required to prototype a new expert system. The right software for the job can save the purchaser many hours of development time. It pays to shop around for the right development software. The more complex the application, the more likely the utility, or other organization, will be to hire a consultant to assist with development.

Cost savings realized through the use of expert systems are desirable, but we might ask, What are some other attractive reasons for investigating AI alternatives? Several possible benefits can emerge, such as:

- *Speed:* Critical plant systems and devices being monitored by human operators can quickly go awry. When things go wrong, expert systems can alert operators in seconds, allowing them to take corrective action to avert a serious problem.

- *Expertise:* Operators get the benefit of an expert opinion, even when no human expert is available.

- *Better Plant Operation:* If an emergency occurs, the main risk facing operators is to correct the problem and handle alarms. This is precisely the time when operators can least afford to divert their attention from plant control.

- *Improved, Uniform Interpretation:* In the case of a nuclear power plant, emergency action levels (EALs) that define the four classifications of emergencies — unusual event, alert, site area emergency, and general emergency — are subject to interpretation. The expert system represents a strict interpretation of any gray areas, helping operators decide if a subtlety is questionable.[3]

A World of Applications

From the previous discussion, one can determine that expert systems offer some decided advantages over traditional methods in some well-defined areas, primarily in power plants. Of the articles written about expert systems use in utilities, the most common examples focus on power plants, both nuclear and fossil. The most likely reason for this is that expert systems can show a very quick payback and remarkable results when appropriately applied in this area. As utilities move forward with AI applications, it is safe to say that power plants will continue to be a primary area for applications development, by virtue of the number of internal systems and primary and auxiliary devices present. However, power plants are certainly not the only promising area for development. In order to add another dimension to this study, this section will briefly cover other types of expert system applications, and discuss the possible ramifications for each. Any critique offered is not meant to dissuade or promote expert system development, but rather as a personal observation to stimulate further discussion. This study will begin with an expert system that isn't used in a power plant.

The Load Forecaster

Southern California Edison, one of the top five utilities in the U.S., is building an expert system to predict summer electrical consumption in the greater Los Angeles area. "The Load Forecaster" is intended to anticipate maximum electrical consumption 24 hours in advance of use. Such information is important because utilities need to know the resources for the next day's load. Otherwise, the utility could experience a blackout (no power) or brownout (low-voltage) condition. The engineer in charge of the project is using AI Corp.'s Knowledge Base Management Systems

(KBMS) tools to create the application. KBMS is written in C and is intended for IBM mainframes, on which Edison will run its application.

The engineer interviewed his expert, a senior system operations engineer, for a total of 16 hours and derived 650 rules that govern the prediction of power needs. He claims, "There are fewer than four or five individuals that could do this job...The job has demands unique to Southern California." During the year, the computer's predictions are compared with a human's. The results will be used to fine-tune the system. The $50,000 system should pay for itself after the first summer of use, according to the engineer. [4]

Such a program is viable for decision support, and is an excellent example of nonplant systems that can help foster efficient operation. Making load predictions is difficult for the inexperienced scheduler. There is much to consider, including predicted temperature, humidity, wind speed and direction, precipitation, and cloud cover—all of which affect customer demand and electrical load on facilities. Another factor is seasonal population, such as might be experienced in coastal communities in the summer and southern states in the winter.

Power systems are balanced systems. Supply must always equal demand, or voltage and frequency can decay to the point of system collapse. Power systems are interconnected throughout the United States at a number of locations. If a large generator is unavailable when a heavy load is predicted, a utility must rely on its tie lines with other utilities and higher cost generators to make up the difference in instantaneous supply and demand. Subsequent loss of more generators in a region, due to unexpected failures, can force one or more utilities to implement emergency procedures, which includes the deliberate shedding of customer load to help keep the high-voltage grid stable and in service. *System security*, a condition in which the high-voltage system is stable, and voltage and frequency are within limits, must be maintained, or a blackout could occur.

An expert system used to predict loads is not positioned in line with ultimate decisions or action, rather it is used for decision support. One might call this a parallel arrangement in the decision chain. Many experienced utility managers may therefore concur that it is a safe and useful tool for utilities. The worst case scenario in using such a system would be that it would recommend a schedule and load estimate that is vastly incorrect. In the hypothetical case that the expert system estimate was used exclusively over the human estimate (not very likely) and proved to be grossly incorrect, the utility could stand to lose substantial funds by scheduling and running high-cost generators that were not required to meet the demand. In such a case, the scheduler would likely lose confidence in the prediction capability of the system under the conditions experienced, and perform remedial work on the system to improve the algorithm and/or knowledge base for predicting loads. Another test period would likely follow.

One might ask the question, Well, why bother at all with such a system? Of course, the answer is that such a system would be very useful as a method of cross-checking a human prediction, and could help to speed the entire process of predicting loads. The system could also perform auxiliary functions for the scheduler, which includes preparing generation schedules. Such schedules can be timeconsuming and tedious to prepare when a dozen or more generators must be scheduled, each with its own incremental cost schedule, i.e., run at a specified output level for a specified cost (usually in mils per kilowatt-hour). The system might also assist in compiling regular reports on power consumption, and help planners decide whether system improvements and upgrades to generators and high-voltage lines might be necessary in the coming years. These are all cost beneficial reasons to implement similar systems.

Now, let us look at an expert system being used as both a diagnostic tool and a training tool.

The Gas Turbine Expert System

Power engineers at Jersey Central Power & Light (JCP&L) are using AI for diagnostic analysis of gas turbines, which are essentially a jet engine coupled to a generator shaft. These units are used to generate power during periods of higher demand, and are often called "peaking units."

Diagnosing and troubleshooting problems in gas turbine power plants require a high level of expertise. Unfortunately, many power utility companies do not have experienced technicians available all of the time. Electric Power Research Institute (EPRI) — the research organization for electric utilities — decided to develop and test the usefulness of an expert system for troubleshooting gas turbine problems, and worked with JCP&L (the host utility and plant expert Honeywell, Inc. supplied the user interface), General Electric Co. (which supplied the system expert and gas turbine expert), and ARINC Research Corp. (which determined the effectiveness of the measurements) to develop a system called the Gas Turbine Expert System (GTES).

Since the GTES runs on a PC, it can be transported to the site in a briefcase. The interface unit can be carried to the site by a technician and plugged into a pre-wired data link, which connects the interface unit to the PC-based computer system located in the power plant's control center. GTES is designed to troubleshoot grounding problems with the control and thermocouple systems. These were chosen as the systems to troubleshoot, because they had been the cause of gas turbine alarms and trips — problems that cause the unit to go off line and remain out of service. As a result of using GTES, even an inexperienced technician was able to diagnose a fault, which clearly proves its value to the host utility. Future plans for GTES include diagnostics in turbine startup, which will extend the usefulness of the system.[5]

GTES is an excellent example of how expert systems can be used as both diagnostic and teaching tools. GTES can help companies like JCP&L reduce the impact of the disparity in expertise that exists between their highest skilled technicians and those with less experience. Because time is money when utilities need their generators on line, such a system could quickly pay for itself by enhancing the availability of units that repeatedly trip off line for similar system problems. Once GTES was tested over a broad range of operating conditions and proven effective, then it could be shared with other utilities to solve similar problems.

Thus, GTES is a type of expert system that, when evaluated from the safety and vigilance angles, is both appropriate and recommended for utility operation. Such systems can enhance personnel safety on the job by recommending a step-by-step procedure for resolving a problem, which also helps to steer a technician away from a potentially dangerous condition. This is similar in many ways to using a checklist, but is far more convenient and comprehensive. Probably the most serious problem that could result from the use of GTES is if inexperienced technicians come to rely on the system and fail to learn the task that it recommends, e.g., Why do I connect wire A to terminal C on panel G1? Utilities can overcome this problem by verifying that the technician is competent in the use of the system and is *learning the task independent of the system*. Periodic testing is also recommended.

Lockout Diagnostic Assistant

At Long Island Lighting Company (LILCO), an expert system has been developed to help newer employees at the 438-Megawatt Port Jefferson power plant to diagnose a *lockout* — a condition whereby a protective relay removes a generator from service. Lockouts occur because of component or wiring failures, or a variety of problems at the sub-system level. Control room personnel must identify and correct the problem before a generator is returned to service. Lockouts do not happen often, but replacement costs can approach $45,000/day. Misdiagnosing the cause of the lockout can cause further damage, and make the unit unavailable for an extended period. The losses quickly add up.

LILCO's resident experts were teamed with AGS Information Services in New York to develop the expert system. The result was the *Lockout Diagnostic Assistant*, an expert system that tells the user what equipment should be examined, and what other specialized employees need to be called in or notified. It also asks the user questions and supplies information. As the user answers questions and supplies information, the system builds a decision chain for what happened. Graphics are a part of the system, allowing a user to bring up a picture or diagram of equipment in question.

The Port Jefferson power plant was selected as the site with the greatest probability of success for a knowledge-system application, "primarily because of a number of its senior personnel are nearing retirement," explained the director of the AGS knowledge engineering group, who adds that "knowledge-systems technology can capture the experience, knowledge, and judgment used by critical personnel to make their decisions."[6]

In this application, the consultant worked very closely on-site with the client to develop an expert system that could be later maintained by the client. This is an excellent way for the client to gain confidence in the system and to learn to train others. The system becomes as much a part of plant operations as other diagnostic tools, further increasing its value. Another key element in this application is the issue of frequency of occurrence. Infrequent events make it difficult for utilities to keep staff in a high state of readiness. Management can help minimize this problem by providing an on-site tool, such as an expert system, that can be queried on-demand as part of an ongoing training program for operating personnel. Simulated events can be scheduled as a test for operating staff in order to help maintain their proficiency at working with the system and for dealing with infrequent events, such as generator trips.

The Reactor Emergency Action Level Monitor (REALM)

The final case that will be reviewed in this brief study is the Reactor Emergency Action Level Monitor, or REALM. Realizing the importance of properly handling emergency situations, Consolidated Edison of New York began a program to assist control-room operators at its Indian Point-2 nuclear generating station. The first phase of the program concentrated on better classifying emergency conditions by focusing on the state of fission-product barrier in addition to specific events throughout the plant. Developers at Technology Application Inc., of Jacksonville, Florida, incorporated these guidelines into an expert system. Con Edison and the Electric Power Research Institute sponsored an off-line prototype. Then Con Edison continued the project to develop the on-line version.

REALM reportedly is the first expert system to go on-line at the control center of a nuclear power plant. Its primary function is to suggest an emergency classification based on emergency action levels (EALs). In the event of an emergency declaration, utilities must notify the Nuclear Regulatory Commission (NRC) and state and local authorities within 15 minutes. The EALs that define the four classifications of emergencies — unusual event, alert, site area emergency, and general emergency —

are subject to interpretation. Using REALM, operators not only see the system's decision, but they also can display the logic behind how the system arrived at it. For example, if REALM suggests an "alert" classification, the operators can review the reason, which might be loss of cold shutdown capability. A possible cause might be that the residual heat removal and auxiliary feedwater systems are inoperable. Operators are able to continue analyzing the conclusion in this manner until every decision eventually is broken down into sensor readings. The operator can also use the system to try what-if scenarios a useful feature for training.

"Engineers designed REALM with a very specific goal in mind. While always scanning, REALM only activates when an emergency occurs. Its specificity allows it to handle these infrequent situations very well," according to a senior mechanical engineer at Con Edison.[7]

Vigilant Approach to Development

With the preceding examples, a snapshot has been provided of some of the many applications of expert systems in utilities. With applications still on the drawing board and many being introduced in mission-critical applications environments, what path might utilities (and other industries) follow to help ensure safe and appropriate application of AI and expert systems?

It can be said with accuracy that further development of expert systems will likely take utilities farther into areas of control. That is to say, that since many expert systems have already proven their worth in diagnostic capacities, it is quite natural, that from now on they will move further into control functions in critical applications. As they move in this direction, it will be all the more important for utilities to embrace the notion of verification and validation (V&V), as suggested by Daniel B. Kirk and Joseph A. Naser in their study on V&V methodology for expert systems in nuclear power applications. Some highlights of the study are:

> Verification may be defined as an activity that ensures that the results of successive steps in the software development cycle correctly embrace the intentions of the previous step (the code is verified to ensure that it fully and exclusively

implements the requirements of its superior specification)...and Validation, that testing is a part of the process of ensuring that the software contains the features and performance attributes prescribed by its requirements specifications...Verification and Validation (V&V) is an essential activity for software which performs critical activities such as those found in nuclear power plant applications...Expert systems have a great potential for application in the Nuclear Power Industry however, they cannot be exempted from the requirement for a complete and thorough V&V program, particularly if they are to shift from their current use in a primarily advisory mode to that of a controlling function...Additional work is being initiated to develop methodologies for nuclear plant V&V. This work is being co-sponsored by EPRI and the Nuclear Regulatory Commission. The methodologies developed under this project will be tested on actual expert systems.[8]

Clearly, there is an effort in the works to standardize and model expert system development in critical applications. This will hopefully avert any catastrophic events that might precipitate from unmitigated use of expert systems. Further, there must be continual dialogue among end users, developers, and planners that goes far beyond the interview process for building a knowledge base. Proactive clients, consultants, and practitioners have already taken this route in the development of many diagnostic expert systems. This remains as a fundamental and required practice as new systems are developed that will be placed in control applications.

Is it feasible that a catastrophic event could precipitate from a non-systematic approach to expert systems development? This is likely the case, because we cannot control all development in all areas, nor would it be practical to do so. In their comprehensive book, *Transforming the Crisis-Prone Organization*, authors Therry Pauchant and Ian Mitroff tell us that people

...are particularly prone to the fallacy of technology. For example, radar, designed to increase marine safety, actually triggered an increase of accidents now with the illusion of safety, captains went faster when radar was on board. We are not saying that humanity should go back to a technology-free society. However, we are saying that to use technology from a self-inflated and omnipotent point of view often leads to disasters.[9]

Is it reasonable to say that operators of critical applications could become accustomed to the "convenience" proposed by expert systems? Might we predict a time when the overworked operator might rely too heavily on the analysis of the expert system for proper guidance? Might the absence of one line of code make the expert system an unpredictable tool, such as the misplaced line of code that caused the massive AT&T network failure on January 15, 1990, causing millions of customers to go without service for nine hours?

Managers can take all the necessary precautions to reduce the probability of disaster through effective programs that encourage interaction and sharing of ideas. Such communications among managers, practitioners, and planners can and must take place in a variety of forums throughout the world, using a knowledgeable approach. Practitioners must be self-motivated enough to ensure that the essential elements of planning and development, and verification and validation are a real part of the movement to place expert systems in important applications. It is clear that one should not be as concerned with who writes the model for expert system development ads with the fact that one is developed and adhered to in mission-critical applications.

Expert system software is being offered to the masses by vendors around the world. Many applications development programs provide a wide array of interfacing possibilities, enabling both the expert and the hacker equal access to the development of critical applications. However, not all applications are being developed under the watchful eye of dedicated professionals or under a pre-qualified model. The placement of those applications is the concern of all end-users, and, conceivably, all of us who may be affected by the users' applications.

Certainly, in the spirit of this book, communications will play a major role in safeguarding development and implementation.

Key Points

- *Expert systems* are the result of setting down to computer code the knowledge of a human expert in a given field. They are commonly used for decision support.

- Expert systems are written using a number of applications development tools and languages. Among them are PROLOG, LISP, C, and other languages, some of which are highly proprietary to the developer.

- *Expert system shells* enable the programmer to develop expert systems quickly, using a simplified graphical interface.

- Expert systems can be developed on a broad range of systems, including PCs.

- Many expert systems are developed for existing applications, replacing or complementing them to perform work.

- There are several advantages for implementing expert systems, including speed of information; expertise of the knowledge worker built into the application; better plant operation; and improved and uniform interpretation of data.

- Many expert system programs are designed to be used in decition support roles.

- The vigilant approach to development and use of expert systems includes verification and validation criteria.

Discussion Topics

1.　Discuss the use of expert systems. What, if any, systems are in use in your organization? Is any research underway to place an expert system in operation at your facility? Would such research be of benefit?

2.　Discuss the use of expert systems to communicate an unusual condition or a potentially threatening condition. What are some of the weaknesses or problems associated with the widespread use of expert systems? What are the strengths?

3.　What do you think is keeping expert systems from growing faster than they have in industry?

For an idea, a hypothesis, a theory, or a fact to be of value it must first be communicated to others. Without communication the most powerful and brilliant people in the most resourceful organizations on earth are weakened, and progress ceases. This fact has been validated the world over when disaster strikes and people lose their ability to communicate with others.

Sam Mullen, President, MPS Communications & Planning Services
Author of *Emergency Planning Guide for Utilities* and *Critical Communications: An Operations Guide for Business.* Mullen has developed contingency plans for nearly 200 organizations.

CHAPTER 12

Epilogue:
Critical Balance Maintained

Future View

The reader has been introduced to some of the important areas of mission-critical communications; however, many readers will need to look further and do more to solidify the principles involved in their organization. But, of course, working toward the goal of being an organization that communicates better while conducting mission-critical business can begin right away.

There is a critical balance that should be maintained with respect to communications in the organization. It begins by carefully indoctrinating employees, providing the necessary training so that far-reaching mistakes can be avoided, as well as misunderstandings about responsibility. For example, the employee needs to be aware of his or her role in the workplace as it fits into the mission of the organization.

The balance can tip toward failure and damaging consequences when employees do not fully understand their mission and take their own needs into consideration ahead of the safety and security of the organization and the people it serves. And do not forget the neighbors. When the tanker Exxon Valdez ran aground on the reef and spilled millions of gallons of oil, devastating "the neighbors," —the residents and ecosystems living near the Port of Valdez, Alaska, —the balance of systems and procedures that keep tankers moving safely was breached. In addition, the mission-critical communications that needed to maintain tanker safety were. The delicate balance involved in mission-critical communications, as can now be seen very clearly, must be maintained.

This is why nearly an entire chapter was devoted to the development of contingency plans. The point is not that organizations do not have them, but having them and knowing the implications of what is in them are two different things. I once took a survey in an organization on the number of managers who were familiar with the emergency plans that were held in various areas of their organization. A very disturbing *10%* of the managers knew emergency plans existed, and fewer still what was in them. The management had never made the commitment that is necessary for corporate survival, but also for the survival of the customers that they serve.

If it were only one organization that was guilty of not taking seriously the need for emergency planning, it would be disturbing, but they could probably convince them that they needed to do some remedial work in that area. However, the real problem is that many mission-critical organizations (their management and employees) are largely ignorant of the critical need for emergency plans.

In addition, the majority of colleges and universities do not teach emergency or contingency planning in the mainstream of core studies at the undergraduate or graduate level. Some of the finest learning institutions in America teach the fundamentals of engineering and business very well, but they lack in scope this critical area of study.

Emergency planning is unpopular. People don't want to think about emergencies and disasters happening in their organizations, or to the people they serve. But, as many people know, in the real world they really do happen. It is critical that a group of people in the organization put the resources to work immediately, and does this through the implementaion of very carefully thought out plans.

Our look into the future should also include the implementation of transaction sets for critical jobs and critical tasks performed by people in those jobs. We should explore the specifics of communications in emergency operations in non-traditional areas of our companies. The early chapters of this book offered keys to the development of T-Sets and how they should be included with job design. The investment in developing these instruments may someday avert a disaster. The workplace will take on a new look in organizations, and employees will have to assume responsibilities with fewer experts on staff. It is therefore incumbent on workers to learn to be effective communicators as they carry on critical business for their organizations, minimizing risk through careful adherence to procedures and to the language of the job.

People will be vying for the attention and attentiveness of others in a world overloaded with information.

> Active information is that which is relevant to our lives. It is in contrast to passive information—or all other information we are fed often against our will. Both of these forms of information, but especially passive information, are growing at an exponential rate. This means much more time is spent seeking the active information and shutting out the passive alternative. In either case, the research indicates that, while the ability of the human population to absorb and utilize this information is increasing modestly, the amount of information is rising at an almost alarming rate.[1]

Management will have to have the best communicators on staff in order to help avoid the ramifications of information overload as it applies to getting critical work done. Organizations will need special codes, in some cases, to help receivers understand that what people are sending them is the information that they, in fact, need immediately.

The tricks that advertisers use to grab attention in the media are not where mission-critical communicators want to be looking because they will be part of the information that people will be automatically filtering out. Communicators will need to revise and upgrade systems for communicating critical information so that people will recognize it and know exactly what to do with the information in the pursuit of critical work.

The special codes and tools required in mission-critical communications will need to be maintained and upgraded, and it will be up to managers to devise new, workable systems to replace the ones that are no longer effective. The exciting part of this is that organizations will continue to be in competition with others, so they will have to have the knowledge on their side as well as the skills to carry out the work. Maintaining precise mission-critical communications will be part of the challenge, and readers must never forget that people, and not machines, are still the principal players in mission-critical work.

Endnotes

Chapter 2 Endnotes

1. Note that the terms *switching person, switchman, operator, quali-fied switchman,* and *troubleman* are used in this text to refer to an individual who performs switching (operates high-voltage switches) on the electric power system for a utility. While qualifications vary somewhat for switching personnel, the terms will be used generical-ly in this text to refer simply to a person who performs switching.

   "Operator" is used elsewhere in this book to refer to people who work with devices and systems in a mission-critical work environ-ment.

2. Charles Perrow, *Normal Accidents: Living with High-Risk Technologies* (New York: Basic Books 1984), pp. 4–5.

3. Rudolf Arnheim, *Visual Thinking* (Berkeley and Los Angeles: University of California Press, 1969), p. 257.

Chapter 4 Endnotes

1. *Author's note:* Do not be concerned about not knowing what the electrical devices are in the examples. Listen to what is being said by the people involved. Also take time to consider how these same problems with communications occur in other industries, and in organizations that you are more familiar with or have read about.

2. William F. Glueck, Personnel: *A Diagnostic Approach* (Plano, TX: Business Publications, Inc., 1982), p. 122.

Chapter 5 Endnotes

1. Hans Heine, An Underestimated Workplace Terror: Mobbing was translated from an article by Dr. jur. Georg Wolff (*Managing Office Technology*, May, 1995), p. 42

2. Dix (Editor) "From Madness to Reason", *Network World Collaboration*, Winter 1995, p. 23.

3. Martin Moore-Ede, Fatigue: The hidden culprit, *USA Weekend* magazine, 1993, January 29-31), p.14.

4. Ibid., p. 16.

5. Martin Moore-Ede, *The Twenty-Four-Hour Society* (Reading, MA.: Addison-Wesley Publishing Company, 1993), p. 71.

Chapter 6 Endnotes
1. Federal Emergency Management Agency (FEMA) *Basic Skills in Decision Making and Problem Solving* (Document IG-63/Aug 1983) p. 31.

Chapter 7 Endnotes
1. Amy Wohl, Multimediaís Time Has Come, (Beyond Computing, March/April, 1995) p. 14.

Chapter 8 Endnotes
1. Stephen Bradley, Jerry Hausman, and Richard Nolan, *Globalization, Technology, and Competition.* (Boston: Harvard Business School Press 1993), pp. 229–230.

Chapter 10 Endnotes
1. Robert Horn *Mapping Hypertext.* (Waltham, Mass.: The Lexington Institute, 1989).

2. More information may be obtained from the Information Mapping Corporation, 300 Third Avenue, Waltham MA, 02154.

3. Michael Gelb *Mind Mapping: How to Liberate Your Natural Genius*, (Nightingale-Conant Corp., 1995). Mind Map is a registered trademark of the Buzan Organization.

Chapter 11 Endnotes

1. IBM and OS/2 are registered trademarks of International Business Machines Corporation (herein after, IBM). *Windows* is a trademark of Microsoft Corporation. DOS (Disk Operating System) is a product offered by IBM, Microsoft, and Digital Research Corporation, in various formats and stages of development.

2. S. Pachalag, "Putting Artificial Intelligence to Work in Power Plants, *Electrical World*, October 1989, p. 62.

3. G. Paula, "Expert System Classifies Nuclear-Plant Emergencies", *Electrical World*, May 1990, p. 48.

4. S. Gibson, A. Cortese, "AI System to Monitor Southern Cal Electricity", *Info World*, unknown date and issue, approx. 1992)

5. D. Smith, "Artificial intelligence — today's new design and diagnostic tool". *Power Engineering*, January, 1989, pp. 28-29.

6. Anonymous. "At LILCO, experts may retire, but they leave their brains behind." . *Electrical World*, March, 1992, p. 12.

7. Paula, "Expert System", p. 48.

8. Kirk and Naser, "A Verification and Validation Methodology for Expert Systems in Nuclear Power Applications", *Expert Systems Applications for the Electric Power Industry*, Vol. 1 (New York: Hemisphere Publishing Corporation), pp. 137–157.

9. Pauchant and Mitroff, *Transforming the Crisis-Prone Organization.* (San Francisco: Jossey-Bass, 1992).

Chapter 12 Endnotes

1. Joseph Pelton, Ph.D., *Future View: Communications, Technology and Society in the 21st Century*, (published by the author, Boulder, CO. 1992), pp. 61-62

Index

DATE DUE

OCT 1 1 '06			
FEB 2 4 2005			
MAY 2 1 2006			
GAYLORD			PRINTED IN U.S.A.